houses of asia

casas asiáticas

case asiatiche

Feierabend

© 2003 Feierabend Verlag OHG
Mommsenstr. 43
D- 10629 Berlin

Traducción del inglés: Silvia Gómez de Antonio & Irene Moreno Palacios
Traduzione dall' inglese: Raffaella Durante-Müller & Eleonora Zoratti
Typesetting of the trilingual edition: adHOC Laureck & Beuster oHG

Editorial director: Kelley Cheng
Art director: Jacinta Neoh
Sub-editors: Hwee-Chuin Ang & Narelle Yakuba
Graphic designers: Chai-Yen Wong & Sharn Selina Lim
Writers/co-ordinators:
Anna Koor (Hong Kong, China)
Barbara Cullen (Melbourne. Australia)
Meng-Ching Kwah (Tokyo, Japan)
Reiko Kasai (Tokyo, Japan)
Richard Se (Kuala Lumpur, Malaysia)
Savinee Buranasilapin (Bangkok, Thailand)
Tatsu Iso (Tokyo, Japan)
Thomas Dannecker (Bangkok, Thailand)

Colour separation: SC Graphic Technology Pte Ltd

Within Small Homes
First published in Singapore in 2003
by Page One Publishing Private Limited
Text & Photography © copyright 2003 Page One Publishing Private Limited
Printing and Binding: Stampa Nazionale s.r.l., Florence

Printed in Italy
ISBN 3-936761-28-0
37 07018 1

On the cover
Photography by Geoff Ang / Courtesy of ISH magazine

houses of asia

casas asiáticas

case asiatiche

Feierabend

contents
sumario
sommario

contents
sumario
sommario

introduction
introducción
introduzione

As our cities become more populated and dense, our dwelling spaces are becoming smaller and smaller. In the most crowded of cities, such as Hong Kong or Tokyo, an entire apartment may only be the size of a single room in a more spacious home elsewhere. Such spatial restriction, of course, requires of the architect or designer a great deal of innovation. The homes presented in this book may be restricted in square footage, but they are unlimited in terms of innovation, style and practicality. They show exciting new ways to conceptualise and configure spaces within small homes for ultimate flexibility and full maximisation of space. With rich colour photographs and descriptive and analytical text, this book shows fifty homes im the Asian and Pacific region, which range from a tiny 330 square foot apartment in Hong Kong, to a Mies van der Rohe-inspired architect's house situated in a lush forest outside Bangkok. The reader is introduced to a variety of houses ranging from free-standing dwellings, apartments, terrace houses and shophouses, to recycled spaces such as converted industrial warehouses and medical clinics. Varied in type they may be, but lacking in innovation they are not.

The benefits of small homes are many: they are cheaper, are easier to upkeep, use less energy and are very cosy. Compact and efficient, they offer inspiration for the maximisation of space, and illustrate ingenious methods for dividing space by using light and furnishings to the greatest advantage. Small Homes shows, above all, that bigger does not necessarily mean better.

A medida que aumenta la población y la densidad de las ciudades, nuestras viviendas pasan a ser cada vez más pequeñas. En las ciudades más habitadas, como por ejemplo en Hong Kong o en Tokio, todo un apartamento puede ser del mismo tamaño que una sola habitación de una casa más amplia en cualquier otro lugar. Estas restricciones de espacio, como es lógico, exigen del arquitecto o del diseñador una gran dosis de innovación. Las viviendas que se presentan en este libro pueden ser limitadas en lo que se refiere al número de metros cuadrados, pero son ilimitadas en cuanto a innovación, estilo y sentido práctico. Nos enseñan nuevas y atractivas formas de concebir y configurar los espacios en el interior de las casas pequeñas para lograr así una mayor flexibilidad y aprovechar al máximo el espacio disponible. A partir de unas fotografías de gran colorido y de un texto analítico y descriptivo, este libro muestra cincuenta hogares ubicados en la región asiática y del Pacífico, desde un diminuto apartamento de 30 metros cuadrados en Hong Kong, hasta la casa de un arquitecto inspirada en Mies van der Rohe y situada en una exuberante selva a las afueras de Bangkok. Al lector se le presentan una gran variedad de viviendas que abarcan desde casas independientes, apartamentos, casas adosadas y casas estilo shophouse, hasta espacios reciclados, tales como almacenes industriales y clínicas reconvertidos. Es probable que sean de muy variados tipos, pero innovación desde luego no les falta.

Son muchas las ventajas de las casas pequeñas: son más baratas, mucho más fáciles de limpiar, gastan menos energía y resultan muy acogedoras. El espacio mínimo y la rentabilidad sirven de estímulo para tratar de aprovechar al máximo el espacio disponible, y muestran ingeniosos métodos para dividir el espacio de la mejor forma posible, por medio de la iluminación y el mobiliario. Casas pequeñas pone de manifiesto, sobre todo, que l o más grande no siempre tiene que ser lo mejor.

Sin dubbio, il momento in cui le nostre città si trasformate in metropoli densamente popolate, i nostri spazi abitativi si sono ristretti sempre più. Nelle città più affollate, come per esempio Hong Kong o Tokyo, un intero appartamento può arrivare ad avere le stesse dimensioni che ha un'unica stanza di una casa più spaziosa altrove. Tale restringimento degli spazi esige da parte di architetti e designer naturalmente grande fantasia e inventiva. Le case presentate in questo libro sono sì molto piccole da un punto di vista del metraggio, ma sono enormi dal punto di vista dell'innovazione, dello stile e della praticità. Mostrano nuovi interessanti modi per progettare e concepire gli interni di case piccole con la massima flessibilità e ottimizzazione degli spazi. Corredato da fotografie colorate e da un commento descrittivo e analitico, questo libro presenta cinquanta casette nella regione asiatica e del Pacifico, a partire da un appartamentino di 30,65 metri quadrati ad Hong Kong, per arrivare a una casa abitata da architetti e ispirata a Mies van der Rohe, situata in una foresta lussureggiante di fronte a Bangkok. Al lettore viene presentata una varietà di case, che va da abitazioni a se stanti, appartamenti, villette a schiera e locali di cui si vogliono riciclare gli spazi, come per esempio vecchi magazzini o cliniche mediche trasformati in abitazioni. Le tipologie sono varie e non mancano le idee innovative.

Sono molti i pregi delle case piccole: sono più economiche, più facili da curare, comportano meno spese e sono molto intime. Piccole e funzionali, offrono ispirazione per l'ottimizzazione degli spazi e mostrano ingegnosi metodi per suddividerli e contemporaneamente ricavare da essi il massimo, grazie all'uso della luce e dell'arredamento. Piccole abitazioni dimostra soprattutto che più grande non significa necessariamente migliore.

albert park house

An extension to an existing single storey weatherboard Edwardian house was an exercise in tight, dense planning. A severe orthogonal idiom has created a new house co-existing along-side the old.

casa en albert park

La ampliación de una antigua casa eduardiana de madera y de una sola planta fue toda una labor de estricta e intensa planificación. Con un austero diseño ortogonal se ha logrado crear una nueva casa que coexiste con la antigua.

casa albert park

L'ampliamento di una casa eduardiana fino al piano di sgrondo dell'unico piano, ha richiesto una progettazione difficile e impegnativa. Uno stile severamente ortogonale ha creato una nuova casa adiacente a quella preesistente.

PROJECT LOCATION **MELBOURNE, AUSTRALIA**
FLOOR AREA **2152 SQFT / 200 SQM**
ARCHITECT / DESIGNER **NICHOLAS GIOIA, RODGER SMITH, NICHOLAS DOUR / NICHOLAS GIOIA**
MAIN PHOTOGRAPHER **TREVOR MEIN**
TEXT **NARELLE YABUKA**

This house compromises two elements: The Edwardian front half of the house was inexpensively restored. This part of the house includes the master bedroom, guest bedroom, formal sitting room and a study. It is the quiet and rather formal part of the house, which also allows the owners a backdrop for their pre-20th century furniture. The modern back of the house has two storeys and is different from the front. The ground floor includes the kitchen, dining and living areas and the main bathroom, the laundry and the ensuite to the master bedroom. The upper level offers two children bedrooms, another bathroom, a recreation area, as well as a storage room.

Esta casa es una combinación de dos elementos: La mitad delantera de la casa, de estilo eduardiano, se restauró sin un coste elevado. Esta parte de la casa incluye el dormitorio principal, el dormitorio de invitados, un salón de diseño formal y un estudio. Es la zona sobria y más bien formal de la casa, que además proporciona a los propietarios un telón de fondo para su mobiliario, anterior al siglo XX. La parte trasera de la casa, más moderna, tiene dos plantas y es distinta de la delantera. La planta baja consta de la cocina, el comedor, la sala de estar y el cuarto de baño principal, el lavadero y el cuarto de baño en suite del dormitorio principal. La planta de arriba ofrece dos dormitorios para los niños, otro cuarto de baño, una zona de juegos y un trastero.

Questa casa è composta da due elementi: il fronte eduardiano della casa era stato restaurato a buon mercato. E' in questa parte che si trovano la camera da letto principale, quella degli ospiti, il salotto di rappresentanza e uno studio. E' la zona della casa più tranquilla e formale, che regala ai proprietari l'ambiente ideale per il loro arredamento risalente a prima del XX sec. Il retro moderno della casa è composto da due piani ed è diverso dal fronte. Al piano terra si trova la cucina, la zona pasti e soggiorno, il bagno principale, la lavanderia e i corridoi che portano alla camera da letto principale. Al piano superiore ci sono due camere per bambini, un altro bagno, una zona gioco e un ripostiglio.

fitzroy terrace house

The fall of a long, narrow site has facilitated the extenson of space from an existing terrace house.

casa adosada en fitzroy

El derrumbe de un solar largo y estrecho ha permitido ampliar el espacio de una casa adosada.

casetta a schiera fitzory

L'abbattimento di una zona della casa lunga e stretta ha facilitato l'ampliamento di una casetta a schiera già esistente.

PROJECT LOCATION **MELBOURNE, AUSTRALIA**
ARCHITECT / DESIGNER **SHELLEY PENN ARCHITECT**
PHOTOGRAPHER **PETER CLARKE**
TEXT **NARELLE YABUKA**

This project involved alterations as well as extensions to an existing terrace house in inner urban Melbourne. The ground floor space is lit by reflected and filtered light that enters through skylights between ceiling planes and windows. The play of light has a fascinating effect. The first floor level offers a studio and sun deck, which are reached via a narrow staircaise. Both are set low amongst the rooftops with the intention to create an intimate and private space rather than to capture the view. Here, the space is flooded by natural light in contrast to the relative seclusion below.

Este proyecto consistió en modificar y ampliar una casa adosada situada en el centro urbano de Melbourne. La planta baja recibe la iluminación de la luz reflejada y filtrada que entra a través de los tragaluces abiertos entre los planos del techo y las ventanas. El juego de luces produce un efecto fascinante. La primera planta consta de un estudio y una terraza, a los que se accede por unas estrechas escaleras. Ambos están situados a baja altura, entre los tejados, con la intención de crear un espacio íntimo y privado, más que de captar las vistas. Aquí, el espacio queda inundado por la luz natural, en contraste con la relativa reclusión de la planta inferior.

Questo progetto ha portato al restauro e all'ampliamento di una casa a schiera già esistente nel pieno centro di Melbourne. La zona al piano terra è illuminata da luce riflessa e filtrata che entra da lucernari posti tra le travi del soffitto e da vetrate. Il gioco di luce ha un effetto affascinante. Al primo piano si trovano uno studio e una terrazza, raggiungibili attraverso una stretta scala. Ambedue sono stati posti al di sotto del tetto con l'intenzione di creare una zona privata e intima, piuttosto che attirare gli sguardi. Lo spazio è qui inondato dalla luce naturale e contrasta con la relativa oscurità del piano inferiore.

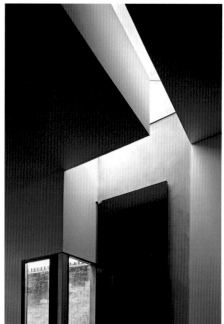

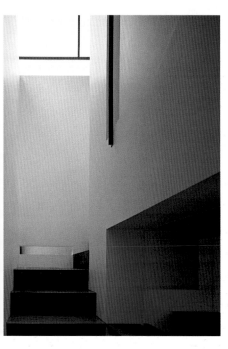

richardson street house

Restraint and elegance were the defining principles for the renovation of this old house, but some sculptural fenestration has given it a fresh expressiveness.

casa en richardson street

El comedimiento y la elegancia fueron los principios básicos a la hora de reformar esta casa antigua; sin embargo, el empleo de algunas ventanas esculturales la dotan de una fresca expresividad.

casa in richardson street

Misura ed eleganza sono i sostantivi più appropriati per definire il restauro di questa vecchia casa, ma la disposizione scultorea di porte e finestre ha regalato anche un aspetto fresco.

PROJECT LOCATION **MELBOURNE, AUSTRALIA**
FLOOR AREA **2454 SQFT / 228 SQM**
ARCHITECT / DESIGNER **NICHOLAS GIOIA, PATRICK GILFEDDER / NICHOLAS GIOIA ARCHITECTS**
PHOTOGRAPHER **TREVOR MEIN**
TEXT **NARELLE YABUKA**

The house is located in a part of Albert Park that was developed in the latter part of the 19th Century. The building has been designed to take full advantage of the site in terms of creating as much interior space as possible, allowing views onto landscaped areas and letting in sunlight. The owner wanted the bedrooms to face the street and the living areas to face a private outdoor living area. As a result, the bathroom and laundry are in the middle, and the kitchen joins the dining and living rooms at the back, facing a secluded courtyard that can also accommodate a car when required. The living areas and the bathroom also face a second courtyard, generously admitting light. The interior, with its calm palette of white walls and timber floors, is brought to life by two windows: a asymmetrical cross, and a round skylight. A circle of light thus elegantly finds its way into the house.

La casa está situada en una parte del Albert Park urbanizada a fines del siglo XIX. El edificio se ha diseñado para sacar el máximo partido del solar y para lograr el mayor espacio interior posible, abriendo las vistas a las zonas ajardinadas y dejando entrar la luz del sol. El propietario deseaba que los dormitorios dieran a la calle, y las salas de estar a un salón privado al aire libre. Como resultado tenemos el cuarto de baño y el lavadero en el centro, y la cocina en la parte posterior, dando al comedor y a la sala de estar y con vistas a un jardín interior cerrado donde, en caso necesario, puede aparcarse un coche. Las salas de estar y el cuarto de baño dan también a un segundo jardín interior, dejando entrar abundante luz. El interior, con su tranquila paleta de paredes blancas y suelos de madera, cobra vida con dos ventanas: una cruz asimétrica y un tragaluz redondo. De esta forma, un círculo de luz hace su elegante entrada en la casa.

La casa è situata in una parte dell'Albert Park, nata e svillupatasi nel tardo XIX sec. L'edificio è stato progettato in modo da trarre il massimo vantaggio dalla sua ubicazione: si è creato uno spazio interno il più ampio possibile, si è aperta la visuale sul paesaggio circostante e si è fatto sì che la luce del sole potesse entrare. I proprietari desideravano le camere da letto sulla strada e la zona soggiorno su una specie di cortile-soggiorno privato. Ne è risultato che il bagno e la lavanderia si trovano nel mezzo e la cucina unisce sala da pranzo e salotto sul retro, di fronte ad un cortile appartato che può fungere anche da parcheggio, se necessario. La zona soggiorno e il bagno affacciano anche su un secondo cortile che immette moltissima luce nella casa. L'interno, con le sue calme tonalità di bianco alle pareti e di legno sui pavimenti è ravvivato da due finestre: una a forma di croce asimmetrica e un lucernario rotondo. Un circolo di luce trova, così, elegantemente la sua via dentro la casa.

richmond warehouse

In a quiet corner of post-industrial Richmond, Melbourne, historic warehouse architecture meets glass-and-metal modernity. Shelley Penn has inserted an objet d'art into this unassuming neighbourhood.

almacén en richmond

En un tranquilo rincón de la zona postindustrial de Richmond, en Melbourne, la histórica arquitectura de naves industriales convive con la modernidad de cristal y metal. Shelley Penn ha insertado un objet d'art en este barrio sin pretensiones.

magazzino richmond

In un angolo tranquillo della Richmond post-industriale, a Melbourne, uno storico magazzino ha incontrato la modernità del vetro e del metallo. Shelley Penn ha inserito un oggetto d'arte in questo quartiere senza pretese.

PROJECT LOCATION MMELBOURNE, AUSTRALIA
ARCHITECT / DESIGNER SHELLEY PENN ARCHITECTS
PHOTOGRAPHER TREVOR MEIN / COURTESY OF SHELLEY PENN ARCHITECTS
TEXT NARELLE YABUKA

This award-winning project is a stunning example of how to combine new and old. The architect has made an addition to the old shell of what was originally one part of a vinegar factory in Richmond, VA. This project involved the conversion of a tiny warehouse shell in to provide a home and painting studio. With brick walls on three sides, the intention was to leave the original shell as ist was and to replace the single timber-framed, eastern wall with a new three-dimensional tower. In deference to the original wall, this is a timber-framed, metal-clad, but light form that offers anintimate atmosphere.

Este galardonado proyecto es un ejemplo sensacional de cómo combinar lo nuevo y lo antiguo. El arquitecto ha realizado una adición a la vieja estructura de lo que en un principio era una parte de una fábrica de vinagre en Richmond, Virginia. Este proyecto supuso la reconversión de una diminuta estructura de un almacén para que sirviera de vivienda y de estudio de pintura. Con paredes de ladrillo en tres lados, lo que se pretendía era conservar tal cual la estructura original y reemplazar la única pared oriental, con entramado de madera, por una nueva torre tridimensional. Por deferencia a la pared original, se trata de una construcción con entramado de madera y revestimiento metálico pero ligera, que ofrece una atmósfera íntima.

Questo è un progetto vincente ed è un meraviglioso esempio del perfetto connubio tra vecchio e nuovo. L'architetto ha creato un prolungamento della struttura di quella che una volta era una parte di una fabbrica di aceto a Richmond. Questo progetto ha comportato la trasformazione di un piccolo magazzino in una abitazione, oltre che nell'atelier di un pittore. Lasciando le pareti su tre lati in mattoni a vista, si voleva mantenere la struttura originale, e si è sostituita solo l'unica parete in legno, sul lato est, con un grande pilastro tridimensionale. Per rispetto alla parete originaria esso è in legno, ma ricoperto in modo delicato da metallo e offre così un'atmosfera intima.

south melbourne house

This project proposes a refreshing prototype for the rejuvenation of a common inner suburban housing type in Australia - the terrace house.

casa en el sur de melbourne

Este proyecto propone un refrescante prototipo para el rejuvenecimiento de un tipo habitual de vivienda en las zonas de los centros urbanos de Australia: la casa adosada.

casa a south melbourne

Questo progetto si propone quale fresco prototipo per dare un'aria nuova ad un tipo di abitazione del tutto comune nel centro suburbano australiano, la villetta a schiera.

PROJECT LOCATION **MELBOURNE, AUSTRALIA**
FLOOR AREA **E1065 SQFT / 99 SQM**
ARCHITECT / DESIGNER **NICHOLAS GIOIA, THOMAS VAKAS / NICHOLAS GIOIA ARCHITECTS**
PHOTOGRAPHER **TREVOR MEIN**
TEXT **NARELLE YABUKA**

With their renovation of this South Melbourne terrace house, Nicholas Gioia Architects have solved some of the common problems of small single-fronted homes such as narrowness, lack of outlook, and claustrophobia. Construction costs were kept down by the use of economical materials and an avoidance of complicated details. Meanwhile, energy consumption is much less than average. All windows are externally shaded to prevent excessive heat gain, and are internally covered to prevent excessive heat loss. Walls and ceilings are insulated to a much greater degree than is required by regulations, and the entire space is heated by one gas heater and two small electric heaters.

Con la reforma de esta casa adosada del sur de Melbourne, Nicholas Gioia Architects han resuelto algunos de los problemas propios de las casas pequeñas de una sola fachada, como la estrechez, la falta de vistas y la claustrofobia. Los gastos de construcción no fueron excesivos, gracias al empleo de materiales económicos y a la ausencia de detalles complicados. Al mismo tiempo, el consumo de energía queda muy por debajo de la media. Todas las ventanas están resguardadas del sol desde el exterior, para evitar que entre demasiado calor, y están protegidas en el interior para evitar pérdidas de calor excesivas. Los niveles de aislamiento de las paredes y los techos superan incluso los exigidos por la normativa legal, y como calefacción para toda la vivienda se utilizan una estufa de gas y dos estufas eléctricas pequeñas.

Con il restauro di questa villetta a schiera nel sud di Melbourne, Nicholas Gioia ha risolto alcuni dei tipici problemi delle case a facciata unica, quali la strettezza, la mancanza di visuale nonché di aria. I costi di costruzione si sono mantenuti bassi grazie all'utilizzo di materiali economici e alla rinuncia a dettagli complicati. Oltre a ciò il consumo energetico è minore che nella media dei casi: tutte le finestre sono oscurate all'esterno per evitare un eccessivo accumulo di calore e sono ricoperte all'interno per evitarne l'eccessiva perdita. Pareti e soffitto sono isolati più di quanto stabilito dalle norme, e l'intera casa è riscaldata da una sola stufa a gas e due piccoli termosifoni elettrici.

apartment in south bay

Having lived in their apartment for almost eight years, the owners decided it was time to rethink their living space from an aesthetic but also pragmatic point of view.

apartamento en south bay

Habiendo vivido en su apartamento durante casi ocho años, los propietarios decidieron que era el momento de dar un cambio a su vivienda desde un punto de vista no sólo estético, sino también pragmático.

appartamento in south bay

I proprietari di questo appartamento, dopo quasi otto anni che ci vivevano, hanno deciso che era giunto il momento di ripensare il suo spazio interno sia da un punto di vista estetico che anche più propriamente funzionale.

PROJECT LOCATION SOUTH BAY, HONG KONG
FLOOR AREA 1500 SQFT / 139 SQM
ARCHITECT / DESIGNER AB CONCEPT LTD
PHOTOGRAPHER EDGAR TAPAN
TEXT ANNA KOOR

One of the primary starting points for the design of this spacious apartment was the owners' passion for crystal glass and the need to display these. By converting the study into a multi-purpose space that also provided areas for storage, the designers were able to solve several issues at once. The entire floor was raised to create an under-floor storage hold. Hinged doors flip-up for access. The open sided box is like a Japanese pavilion: the owners can entertain and demonstrate their displays; a panel opens to reveal a small workstation with all the essential telecommunications.

Uno de los puntos de partida básicos en el diseño de este amplio apartamento fue la pasión de los dueños por el cristal y la necesidad de que quedara a la vista. Transformando el estudio en un espacio multiuso, incluso con sitio para guardar cosas, los diseñadores lograron resolver varias cuestiones al mismo tiempo. Así, todo el suelo se elevó para crear un espacio de almacenamiento subterráneo. Una puertas tipo batiente se levantan para permitir el acceso. La construcción, cúbica y abierta por un lado, se asemeja a un pabellón japonés: los dueños pueden recibir a las visitas y mostrar las estancias; un panel se abre dejando ver un pequeño despacho con todos los elementos básicos de telecomunicación.

Uno dei punti di partenza più importanti per la progettazione di questo spazioso appartamento è stata la passione dei proprietari per il cristallo e il bisogno di metterlo in mostra. Nella trasformazione dello studio in uno spazio multifunzionale, comprendente anche una zona di ripostiglio, gli architetti sono stati in grado di risolvere contemporaneamente diversi problemi. L'intero pavimento è stato rialzato per creare un ripostiglio sotterraneo. Porte a cardini si aprono agli ingressi. La camera aperta ai lati assomiglia ad un padiglione giapponese: il proprietario può ricevere gli ospiti e mostrare loro da lì le sue collezioni di cristallo; un pannello si apre a svelare una piccola zona lavoro con tutti i mezzi di telecomunicazione essenziali.

artist's residencce

This artist's apartment contains no computers, telephones or TVs. Instead, this nest for meditation, rest and sleep contains what could be described as a Rubik's cube in furniture form, with a kitchen that can grow and shrink.

residencia de un artista

En el apartamento de este artista no hay ordenadores, teléfonos ni televisores. En cambio, en este nido para la meditación, el descanso y el sueño encontramos lo que podría describirse como un cubo de Rubik en forma de mobiliario, con una cocina que puede agrandarse o reducirse.

appartamento di artisti

In questo appartamento di artisti non si trovano computer, telefoni o televisori; questo rifugio per la meditazione, il riposo e il sonno, potrebbe anzi essere anche definito un cubo di Kubrik travestito da arredamento, e contiene una cucina in grado di ingrandirsi e rimpicciolirsi.

PROJECT LOCATION **MID LEVELS, HONG KONG**
ARCHITECT / DESIGNER **DRAUGHTZMAN**
PHOTOGRAPHER **KELLEY CHENG**
TEXT **ANNA KOOR**

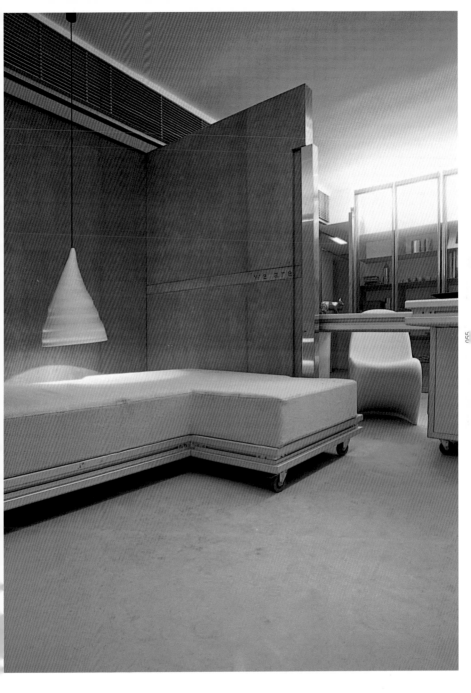

This flat was compartmentalised into a row of three minute bedrooms leading off a dark corridor. One length of the corridor was removed as well as the intervening walls to leave one big living space with three windows overlooking the city. The remaining passageway wall distributes the bathroom amenities and storage. Substituting doors, there are three cement-faced movable walls that glide over the various openings. One of these panels also swings right out, creating a temporary wall across the apartment when privacy is needed. The singular piece of furniture in the centre of the room is like Rubik's cube. It can be remodeled for every opportunity – for sleeping, eating, studying.

Este piso estaba dividido en tres minúsculos dormitorios que daban a un pasillo oscuro. Una parte del pasillo se suprimió, así como las paredes intermedias, para dejar una gran sala con tres ventanas con vistas al centro de la ciudad. A lo largo del resto de la pared del pasillo se distribuyen el cuarto de baño y el trastero. En lugar de puertas, hay tres paredes móviles recubiertas de cemento que se deslizan sobre las distintas aberturas. Uno de estos paneles también puede girarse hacia afuera, creando una pared provisional a lo ancho del apartamento para cuando se precise intimidad. El mueble tan peculiar ubicado en el centro de la estancia es como el cubo de Rubik. Puede adoptar diversas formas según la ocasión: para dormir, comer o estudiar.

Questo appartamento era suddiviso in una fila di tre minuscole camere da letto che partiva da uno scuro corridoio. Una parete del corridoio era stata abbattuta, così come anche le pareti divisorie delle stanze e si era quindi creata un'unica grande camera con tre finestre con vista sulla città. Sulla restante parete del corridoio si aprono il bagno e il ripostiglio. Le porte sono state sostituite da tre grandi pannelli scorrevoli ricoperti di cemento in grado da fungere da porta per tutte le aperture della casa. Uno di questi pannelli può addirittura essere sganciato e trasformato in parete divisoria posta nel mezzo dell'appartamento, qualora sia necessaria un po' di privacy. Questo pezzo singolare d'arredamento al centro è una specie di cubo magico, può essere spostato o rimesso a posto a seconda che si voglia dormire, mangiare o studiare.

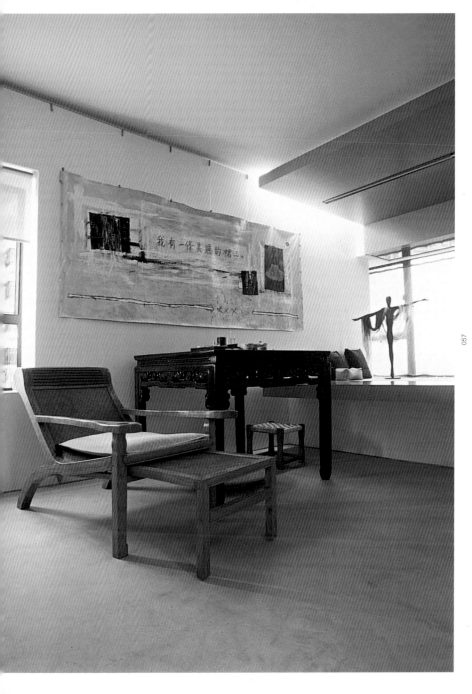

we are the artwork of GOD

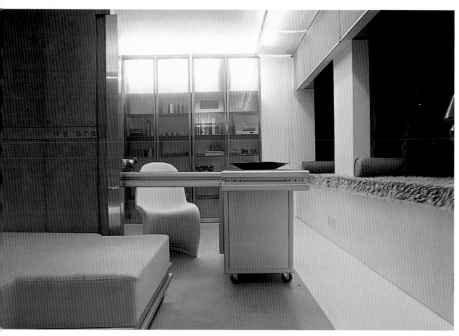

059

we are   the artwork of GOD

bachelor residence

Proportion, light and scale are captured and manipulated in the renovation of this bachelor's apartment. The result is a theatrical space of movement, compression and release.

residencia de soltero

En la reforma de este apartamento de soltero se han dominado y manipulado la proporción, la luz y la escala. El resultado es un espacio teatral de movimiento, compresión y liberación.

appartamento da scapolo

Nel restauro di questo appartamento da scapolo si sono prese in considerazione proporzioni, luce e metraggio e con essi si è giostrato fino a raggiungere come risultato una specie di palcoscenico, su cui ci si può muovere, concentrare e rilassare.

PROJECT LOCATION **MID LEVELS, HONG KONG**
FLOOR AREA **930 SQFT / 86 SQM**
ARCHITECT / DESIGNER **ANDRE FU OF AFSO DESIGN**
PHOTOGRAPHER **JOHN BUTLIN / KELLEY CHENG**
TEXT **ANNA KOOR**

In this apartment, the architect's intention was to create a sanctuary for modern urban living. Fortunately, the absence of structural walls presented the opportunity to open out the space, and create a panorama of the spectacular views, instead of a fragmented outlook. The result is a symmetrical volume that combines living, dining, working and resting functions. Each of them can be used simultaneously and without disrupting other areas. The central bulkhead, which serves as a conduit for lighting, is clad in steel, reducing its mass with its subtle reflectivity. Pietra di Lecce limestone, solid ash furniture and plastered surfaces provide a counterpoint to steel and the smoked glass between the end of the bed and the dining table.

En este apartamento, la intención del arquitecto era crear un santuario para la vida urbana moderna. Por suerte, la ausencia de muros estructurales permitió ensanchar el espacio y crear una visión panorámica de las espectaculares vistas, en vez de una visión fragmentada. El resultado es un volumen simétrico que combina las funciones de residencia, comedor y lugar de trabajo y de descanso. Cada una de estas zonas puede emplearse simultáneamente, sin perjuicio del resto. El tabique central, que sirve de conducto para la luz, está recubierto de acero, de forma que su tamaño parece reducirse al reflejar suavemente la luz. El empleo de piedra caliza del tipo Pietra di Lecce, el mobiliario realizado en sólida madera de fresno y las superficies enyesadas proporcionan un contrapunto al acero y al vidrio ahumado entre el extremo de la cama y la mesa del comedor.

L'intenzione dell'architetto in questo appartamento era quella di creare un santuario del vivere cittadino moderno. Per fortuna l'assenza di pareti portanti ha permesso di aprire gli spazi creando un palcoscenico per un panorama fantastico, invece di spezzettare la visuale. Il risultato è un ambiente simmetrico che combina il soggiorno, la zona pasti, quella lavoro e tutte le altre. Ognuna di esse può essere utilizzata contemporaneamente e senza che si crei disturbo per le altre zone. La paratia centrale che conduce la luce è ricoperta in acciaio e riduce il proprio volume grazie ad un gioco di riflessi. Pietra calcarea di Lecce, mobili di lava e superfici intonacate fanno da contraltare al pannello in acciaio e vetro satinato tra i piedi del letto e il tavolo da pranzo.

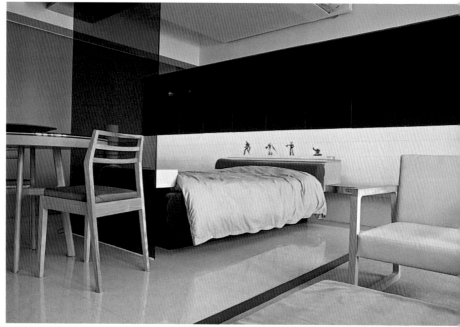

bertrand/lee apartment

A new wall that cuts right through this photographer's apartment frames views and spaces into focus.

apartamento de bertrand/lee

Un nuevo muro que atraviesa el apartamento de este fotógrafo sirve para enmarcar las vistas y los espacios en un primer plano.

appartamento bertrand/lee

Una nuova parete che taglia questo appartamento, appartenente ad un fotografo, concentra sguardi e camere al centro.

PROJECT LOCATION **MID-LEVELS, HONG KONG**
FLOOR AREA **970 SQFT / 90 SQM**
ARCHITECT/DESIGNER **FRANK CHIU/ONE: CHINA STUDIO**
PHOTOGRAPHER **VIRGILE SIMON BERTRAND**
TEXT **ANNA KOOR**

Despite a modest, segregated floor space and a tight budget, this apartment has undergone an impressive renovation. A cross-wall which cut the flat in half was removed to gain the third bedroom and also creating more space, light and harbour views. A new wall was constructed which was to be the singular element of the room. The apartment has its own lobby and this is where the wall starts, from the front door in a straight line until it hits the end elevation. The architect's method was to re-align the geometry of the flat. Kitchen, dining, bedroom, bathroom, sofas, bookcase are located perpendicular to the wall to underline its presence.

A pesar de lo modesto y segregado del espacio y de lo ajustado del presupuesto, este apartamento ha experimentado una admirable reforma. La pared que dividía el piso por la mitad se suprimió para ganar una tercera habitación y lograr más espacio, iluminación y vistas al puerto. Se construyó una pared nueva, que se convirtió en el elemento más singular de la habitación. El apartamento tiene su propio vestíbulo, desde el que se inicia el muro, construido en línea recta desde la puerta delantera hasta alcanzar su altura final. El arquitecto optó por el método de realinear la geometría del apartamento. La cocina, el comedor, el cuarto de baño, los sofás y la estantería están situados perpendiculares a la pared, para resaltar su presencia.

A dispetto dello spazio ristretto e chiuso e dei pochi mezzi a disposizione, questo appartamento ha subito un restauro veramente impressionante. Una parete che divideva l'appartamento a metà era stata abbattuta per poter ricavare una terza camera da letto, creare maggior spazio, luce e visuale. E' stata poi costruita una nuova parete che doveva essere l'unico elemento della stanza. L'ingresso dell'appartamento si trova proprio dove inizia la parete, dalla porta centrale diritto fino ad arrivare alla fine della parete stessa. L'architetto ha praticamente riallineato la geometria dell'appartamento. Cucina, sala da pranzo, camera da letto, bagno, divani, scaffali, sono tutti posti perpendicolarmente alla parete a sottolinearne la presenza.

gary's apartment

With a compact and efficient layout of dual function space and concealed storage, this minuscule apartment manages to attain an attractive ambience for its occupant.

apartamento de gary

Con la distribución mínima y bien aprovechada de un espacio bifuncional y un trastero oculto, este minúsculo apartamento consigue un ambiente atractivo para su ocupante.

appartamento di gary

Col suo aspetto compatto ed efficiente e le due funzioni di spazio abitativo e ripostiglio nascosto, questo minuscolo appartamento diventa un ambiente estremamente interessante per chi ci vive.

PROJECT LOCATION **ISLAND EAST, HONG KONG**
FLOOR AREA **330 SQFT / 31 SQM**
ARCHITECT / DESIGNER **EDGE (HK) LTD**
PHOTOGRAPHER **ALMOND CHU**
TEXT **ANNA KOOR**

The minute apartment belongs to a bachelor accomodating his lifestyle and daily routine. Squeezing the normal functions of a home into this amount of space was only possible through the strategy of making spaces perform multiple roles. An efficient arrangement of kitchenette, bathroom and laundry area liberates the remaining space to fulfill other life necessities. The space is dominated by white, transparent materials. A full-height tower intersects the space, built in solid cherry wood. This object accommodates the movie projector, refrigerator, kitchen, basin and the laundry. Elsewhere, space is utilised through means of partitions, light and mobile furniture. The need for storage has been solved by sorting books, CDs, clothes, stereo, etc into a chrome factory shelving system. This leaves the central space free for resting, working, dressing, reading, sleeping, and eating.

El minúsculo apartamento pertenece a un soltero y está acondicionado para su estilo de vida y su rutina diaria. Conseguir incluir las funciones típicas de una vivienda dentro de esta cantidad de espacio sólo fue posible mediante la estrategia de diseñar los espacios para que cumplieran distintos cometidos. La acertada disposición de la cocina americana, del cuarto de baño y del lavadero deja libre el espacio restante para destinarlo a las demás necesidades. El espacio está dominado por el color blanco y por los materiales transparentes. Una torre hasta el techo, construida en madera maciza de cerezo, cruza el espacio. Este objeto sirve para colocar el proyector de cine, la nevera, la cocina, el lavabo y el lavadero. En el resto del apartamento, el espacio se aprovecha gracias a las particiones y al mobiliario ligero y móvil. La necesidad de un espacio para guardar ordenados los libros, los CDs, la ropa, el equipo de música, etc. se ha resuelto empleando un sistema de estanterías de fábrica en cromo. De esta forma, en el centro de la estancia queda libre un espacio para descansar, trabajar, vestirse, leer, dormir y comer.

Questo minuscolo appartamento è la soluzione ideale per le esigenze dello stile di vita di uno scapolo e la sua routine quotidiana. Ricavare le normali funzioni di una casa in questo piccolo spazio è stato possibile solamente adibendo i diversi spazi a più funzioni. Una progettazione studiata per angolo cottura, bagno e lavanderia, ha fatto sì che restasse spazio per altre esigenze. Tutto è dominato dal bianco e da materiali trasparenti. Una colonna in solido legno di ciliegio taglia lo spazio. Qui troviamo il proiettore, il frigo, la cucina, il lavello e la zona lavanderia. Il restante spazio è occupato da pannelli divisori, luci e mobili. Un sistema di scaffalature in cromo adempie ai bisogni di riporre libri, CD, vestiti, stereo... In questo modo lo spazio centrale viene lasciato libero per il riposo, il lavoro, per vestirsi, leggere, dormire e mangiare.

ken rose apartment

Culinary and musical passions were the definitive influences on the design of this flexible apartment for a jazz musician.

apartamento de ken rose

La pasión por la cocina y por la música influyó de forma decisiva en el diseño de este apartamento acondicionado para un músico de jazz.

appartamento ken rose

La passione per la cucina e la musica sono stati i punti di partenza per la progettazione di questo flessibile appartamento per un musicista jazz.

PROJECT LOCATION **MID LEVELS, HONG KONG**
FLOOR AREA **900 SQFT / 84 SQM**
ARCHITECT / DESIGNER **JASON CAROLINE DESIGN LTD / ARCHITUDE STUDIO**
PHOTOGRAPHER **ANDREW CHESTER ONG**
TEXT **ANNA KOOR**

The apartment's owner is a professor and jazz musician. He and his wife chose to live in a traditional neighbourhood with easy access to the hub of Hong Kong's nightlife. The owner's profession called for a number of stipulations in relation to the design. The living room had to measure the exact dimensions for acoustic perfection. Storage was needed for the vast music collection, also a practice room. The architects' intention was to play with the dimensions and the relationship between spaces. This home can resemble to an area completely open like a loft. The center piece is the bathroom, which itself de-materialises on opposite sides when frosted glass openings are pushed back. It is almost a free-standing element, denoted with raw concrete. Its permeability allows views through the apartment. More importantly, during the day, natural light filters through the space and at night, the opposite occurs when the bathroom becomes a self-illuminated light box.

El propietario del apartamento es profesor y músico de jazz. Él y su mujer decidieron vivir en un barrio tradicional, con fácil acceso al epicentro de la vida nocturna de Hong Kong. La profesión del dueño planteó una serie de exigencias en lo referente al diseño. La sala de estar tenía que tener las dimensiones exactas para lograr una acústica perfecta. Era preciso contar con un espacio para guardar la gran colección de música, y una sala para ensayar. El propósito del arquitecto era jugar con las dimensiones y con la relación entre los espacios. Esta casa puede parecerse a un área totalmente abierta, como un loft. La pieza central es el cuarto de baño, que parece desvanecerse en los lados opuestos cuando se cierran las puertas de cristal esmerilado. Es casi un elemento independiente cuya presencia es resaltada por el hormigón en bruto. Su permeabilidad permite ver el apartamento y, lo que es aún más importante, durante el día la luz natural se filtra a través del espacio, mientras que de noche sucede todo lo contrario, y el cuarto de baño se convierte en un cubo luminoso.

Il proprietario dell'appartamento è un professore e musicista jazz. Lui e sua moglie hanno scelto di vivere in un quartiere tradizionale da cui è facile raggiungere il cuore della vita notturna di Hong Kong. La professione del proprietario ha richiesto che ci si accordasse bene durante la progettazione. Le dimensioni del soggiorno dovevano essere tali da offrire un'acustica perfetta. Era necessario spazio, una vera e propria stanza per le varie collezioni di dischi e CD. L'architetto si era prefisso di giostrare con le dimensioni e le relazioni tra gli spazi. Questa abitazione può essere paragonata a un unico grande spazio abitativo aperto, come un attico. La parte centrale è costituita dal bagno che scompare dall'altra parte se si spingono indietro le porte in vetro satinato. Esso è anche un elemento a se stante messo in risalto dal cemento grezzo. La sua permeabilità consente diverse visuali dell'appartamento. In modo più significativo, durante il giorno, la luce naturale filtra attraverso di esso e di notte, succede il contrario, perché il bagno si trasforma praticamente in una specie di lampada.

paul hicks apartment

His traveling has fed Paul Hicks with some great ideas for the interior of his apartment.

apartamento de paul hicks

Los viajes le han proporcionado a Paul Hicks grandes ideas para el interior de su apartamento.

appartamento paul hicks

Durante i suoi viaggi Paul Hicks ha raccolto bellissime idee per il suo appartamento.

PROJECT LOCATION **MID LEVELS, HONG KONG APARTMENT**
FLOOR AREA **900 SQFT / 84 SQM**
ARCHITECT / DESIGNER **BHI LTD**
PHOTOGRAPHER **JOHN BUTLIN**
TEXT **ANNA KOOR**

The location was the chief factor when Hicks was searching for his new abode, primarily because he prefers the different facets of his life (work, socialising, shopping) to be right outside the front door. Another priority was that the apartment needed to be everything at all times: a place to catch up with work or catch up with sleep; a place to retreat and relax; and a place to entertain both formally and casually, for friends to drop by and hang out. Designer Bruce Harwood has created an introverted space roughly divided into quadrants denoting living room, bedroom, bathroom and kitchen. An unobtrusive wall-to-wall self-illuminating closet lines the back wall, which is home to all Hicks' storage needs. The open kitchen maintains visual uniformity and a backlit glass half-wall forms a glowing interface between bedroom and living room.

La ubicación fue para Hicks el factor principal a la hora de buscar su nueva vivienda, sobre todo porque prefiere tener las distintas facetas de su vida (el trabajo, las relaciones, las compras) justo a la puerta de casa. Otra prioridad era que el apartamento tenía que ser todo a todas horas: un lugar para ponerse al día con el trabajo o para recuperar horas de sueño; un lugar para retirarse y descansar, un lugar para recibir a invitados, ya sea de modo formal o informal, para que los amigos puedan pasarse un momento o puedan quedarse más tiempo. El diseñador Bruce Harwood ha creado un espacio «introvertido», dividido de modo aproximado en cuadrantes para conformar la sala de estar, el dormitorio, el cuarto de baño y la cocina. Un discreto armario empotrado con iluminación interior cubre la pared trasera y resuelve todas las necesidades de almacenamiento de Hicks. La cocina abierta sirve para mantener la uniformidad visual, y una semipared de vidrio a contraluz es una iluminada zona de transición entre el dormitorio y la sala de estar.

La posizione è stato il fattore più importante quando Hicks ha cercato la sua nuova abitazione, in primo luogo perché egli ritiene che i vari aspetti della sua vita (lavoro, amicizie, acquisti) debbano svolgersi al di fuori delle mura domestiche. Un altro presupposto era che l'appartamento avrebbe dovuto essere tutto contemporaneamente: un posto in cui poter lavorare e dormire, in cui poter ritirarsi e riposarsi; un posto in cui accogliere ospiti e amici, per invitarli, nonché un posto in cui vivere. L'architetto Bruce Harwood ha creato uno spazio chiuso in sé stesso diviso approssimativamente in quadrati che rappresentano il soggiorno, la camera da letto, il bagno e la cucina. Uno spazio discreto e autoilluminato prende tutta la parete posteriore e regala a Hicks un perfetto ripostiglio. Una cucina aperta mantiene l'uniformità della visuale e una mezza parete in vetro forma una luminosa barriera tra camera da letto e soggiorno.

peak apartment

Living the life of a minimalist is often easier said than done, particularly for a family.

apartamento en peak

Suele ser más fácil hablar de minimalismo que ponerlo en práctica, en particular para una familia.

appartamento peak

Vivere da minimalisti è più facile a dirsi che a farsi, specie per un'intera famiglia.

PROJECT LOCATION **THE PEAK, HONG KONG**
ARCHITECT / DESIGNER **KplusK ASSOCIATES**
PHOTOGRAPHER **GRAHAM UDEN**
TEXT **ANNA KOOR**

The pursuit of perfection through simplifying form and material has to be poised against practical realities. The owners had every intention of achieving the former. As is typical of K plus K's interior endeavours, every non-structural element in the apartment was erase. With spectacular views of ocean and lush forest flanking both long elevations, the mean-windowed facades were punched out and enlarged into single glazed openings. The master bedroom in this apartment has unusually close proximity to the kitchen and family activities, but can revert to a private sanctuary when required. Throughout the apartment, devices are created to hide extraneous equipment, light switches, surround-sound speakers, computers, blinds, and so on.

La búsqueda de la perfección simplificando la forma y el material tiene que tener en cuenta las realidades prácticas. Los propietarios estaban totalmente decididos a lograr esa perfección. Tal y como es habitual en los proyectos de diseño para interiores de K plus K, se han suprimido del apartamento todos los elementos superfluos. Con espectaculares vistas al océano y a la exuberante selva flanqueando ambas fachadas, las diminutas ventanas se ampliaron perforando sencillas aberturas de vidrio. En este apartamento el dormitorio se encuentra más cerca de lo acostumbrado de la cocina y del resto de habitaciones comunes, pero puede volver a convertirse en un santuario privado cuando sea preciso. Por todo el apartamento se han empleado una serie de recursos para ocultar los elementos superfluos, los interruptores de la luz, los altavoces de sonido envolvente, los ordenadores, las persianas, etc.

La ricerca della perfezione attraverso la semplificazione di forme e materiali va soppesata con la realtà pratica. Il proprietario di questo appartamento aveva tutte le intenzioni di raggiungere appunto la perfezione. Secondo la tipiche idee guida di K plus K, sono state eliminate tutte le pareti dell'appartamento che non fossero portanti. Data la vista spettacolare sull'oceano e sulla foresta lussureggiante da entrambi i lati della casa, le finestre principali sono state ampliate e le facciate trasformate in grandi vetrate luminose. La camera da letto principale è insolitamente molto vicina alla cucina e altre zone di vita attiva della famiglia, ma può anche tornare a essere un santuario privato se ce ne sia la necessità. Sono stati creati diversi espedienti in tutto l'appartamento per nascondere le apparecchiature estranee quali interruttori delle luci, casse, computer, schermi, ecc.

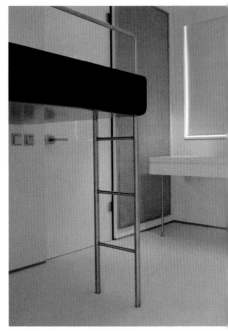

shama apartment 1

Shama stems from an ancient Sanskrit word meaning «tranquility, an oasis of calm» and this sums up what the property group and their designer aimed to deliver to their residents.

apartamento shama 1

El término shama procede de una antigua palabra sánscrita que significaba «tranquilidad, oasis de calma», y esto resume lo que este grupo inmobiliario y su diseñador pretendían proporcionar a sus residentes.

appartamento shama 1

Shama deriva dall'antica parola sanscrita che significa «tranquillità, oasi di calma» e sintetizza perfettamente ciò che il gruppo di proprietari e gli architetti miravano a ottenere per questa abitazione.

PROJECT LOCATION 8 RUSSELL STREET CAUSEWAY BAY, HONG KONG
FLOOR AREA 1,170 SQFT / 109 SQM
ARCHITECT/DESIGNER DILLON GARRIS
PHOTOGRAPHER KELLEY CHENG
TEXT ANNA KOOR

This generously sized apartment was created for a business man who wants all the comfor of home combindes with all the luxuries of a five-star-hotel. It needed to provide a balance between business and personal life whilst celebrating Hong Kong's vibrant lifestyle. Another parameter to the brief was the need to be international in luxury but exude a definite Asian charm. Attention to this detail was overseen directly by the Shama team who regularly travel the world sourcing soft furnishings, textiles, ceramics, linen, original artwork and also floor coverings. However, the attitude is modern Asia rather than anything ethnic. Often, the only clue might be in colour – a ripe aubergine, a vibrant red, or simply the more earthy tones that are akin to Japanese interiors.

Este apartamento de generosas proporciones se creó para un empresario que desea contar en casa con todo el confort combinado con todos los lujos de un hotel de cinco estrellas. Fue necesario lograr un equilibrio entre los negocios y la vida privada, en un canto al estilo de vida efervescente de Hong Kong. Otro factor que se tuvo en cuenta fue la necesidad de ser internacional en cuanto al lujo, pero emanando al mismo tiempo un claro encanto asiático. El cuidado de estos detalles fue supervisado directamente por el equipo Shama, que viaja regularmente por el mundo en busca de delicado mobiliario, textiles, cerámicas, ropa de cama, originales obras de arte y revestimientos para suelos. Sin embargo, la actitud es más asiática moderna que étnica. A menudo, la única pista podría estar en el color: un berenjena oscuro, un rojo vibrante, o sencillamente los tonos más terrosos similares a los de los interiores japoneses.

L'appartamento, molto grande, era stato creato per un uomo d'affari che desiderava unire tutte le comodità di una casa e i lussi di un albergo a cinque stelle. Voleva riuscire a trovare un equilibrio tra vita d'affari, quella privata e onorare contemporaneamente anche il vibrante stile di vita di Hong Kong. Un altro parametro da seguire in questo progetto era il bisogno di un lusso di stile internazionale che lasciasse però percepire chiaramente un determinato charme asiatico. Il team Shama, che girava regolarmente il mondo alla ricerca di tende, tessuti, ceramiche, biancheria, opere d'arte originali e pavimentazioni, si incaricò personalmente di sovrintendere all'adempimento di questi dettagli. Il risultato doveva comunque essere uno stile asiatico moderno piuttosto che qualcosa di etnico. Spesso l'unica indicazione era un colore, color melanzana matura, un vibrante rosso, o semplicemente i diversi toni della terra, propri degli interni giapponesi.

shama apartment 2

If spaces have multiple uses, the comfort of this boutique
living environment is maximised.

apartamento shama 2

Si los espacios tienen múltiples usos, se potencia al máximo
el confort de este entorno residencial de boutique.

appartamento shama 2

Se anche lo spazio è adibito ai più diversi usi, il comfort
di questa specie di boutique del ben vivere è enorme.

PROJECT LOCATION **8 RUSSELL STREET CAUSEWAY BAY, HONG KONG**
FLOOR AREA **730 SQFT / 68 SQM**
ARCHITECT / DESIGNER **DILLON GARRIS**
PHOTOGRAPHER **KELLEY CHENG**
TEXT **ANNA KOOR**

Luxury is not compromised by this fairly modest dimensions of the one-bedroom unit. In fact the planning of this living space positively challenges the assumptions that small is by nature cramped and awkward. There were significant concerns such as the availability of only one window. Lack of light is mitigated by the use of single-ply Thai silk screens which divide the bed from the living quarters. The designer did not hold back on other essentials such as the closet space which is disproportionately generous, a king-size bed with sumptuous linen, and an openly streamlined bathroom.

El lujo no resulta perjudicado por las dimensiones realmente modestas de este apartamento de un dormitorio. De hecho, el diseño de esta vivienda desafía positivamente la asunción de que lo pequeño es, por naturaleza, apretado e incómodo. Hubo una significativa preocupación por la existencia de una única ventana. Para atenuar los efectos de la falta de luz se emplean biombos de seda tailandeses de una lámina, que separan la cama del resto del apartamento. El diseñador no escatimó en el uso de otros elementos esenciales tales como el armario, desproporcionadamente amplio, una cama de matrimonio con suntuosa ropa de cama y un cuarto de baño abiertamente funcional.

Il lusso non è compromesso dalle dimensioni alquanto modeste dell'arredamento componibile dell'unica camera da letto. La progettazione di questo spazio infatti sfida positivamente l'assunzione che spazi piccoli siano per natura limitati e scomodi. C'erano importanti punti da risolvere, quali per esempio la presenza di una sola finestra. La scarsità di luce è stata risolta dall'uso di semplici paraventi di seta thailandese che dividono la zona notte da quella giorno. Il designer non si è limitato neanche quando si trattava di altri particolari, come per esempio quando ha posto nello spazio chiuso della camera da letto un letto sproporzionatamente grande con biancheria estremamente lussuosa, e quando ha progettato il bagno aperto dalla forma aerodinamica.

wong apartment

Sunaqua Concepts have made the most of a small space to provide a comfortable home centred around a collection of books and electronic toys.

apartamento de wong

Sunaqua Concepts ha sacado el máximo partido de un espacio pequeño para lograr un hogar confortable centrado en torno a una colección de libros y juguetes electrónicos.

appartamento wong

Sunaqua Concept ha trasformato la maggior parte degli spazi angusti in una abitazione confortabile, circondata da collezioni di libri e giochi elettronici.

PROJECT LOCATION **TSING YI, HONG KONG**
FLOOR AREA **475 SQFT / 45 SQM**
ARCHITECT / DESIGNER **SUNAQUA CONCEPTS LTD**
PHOTOGRAPHER **DICK**
TEXT **ANNA KOOR**

Overlooking the hulking industrial-scape of Tsing Yi's shipping container terminals, this flat at Villa Esplanada is diminutive in form. The young, newly married couple who owns the apartment embarked on a renovation programme within a very tight budget. Sun Wong from Sunaqua Concepts began the design process by examining his clients' focus of enjoyment, in this case a vast collection of books and electronic toys. The intention was to project the character of the owners and promote comfort and intimacy with their surroundings. Therefore the first objective was to devise a storage and display system suitable for their collections. This is designed as a continuous frame that lines the walls and ceiling between the dining and living areas. The composite structure of raw steel supports a series of suspended open oak timber crates or trays.

Este piso en Villa Esplanada, con vistas al descomunal paisaje industrial de los terminales de contenedores de Tsing Yi, es diminuto. La joven pareja de recién casados propietaria del apartamento se embarcó en un programa de reformas con un presupuesto muy reducido. Sun Wong, de Sunaqua Concepts, inició el proceso de diseño teniendo en cuenta la principal diversión de sus clientes, en este caso una amplia colección de libros y juguetes electrónicos. La intención era proyectar el carácter de los propietarios y potenciar el confort y la intimidad con su entorno. Por lo tanto, el primer objetivo era concebir un sistema adecuado para guardar y exponer sus colecciones. Este se diseñó como un marco continuo que cubre las paredes y el techo entre el comedor y la sala de estar. La estructura compuesta de acero bruto sirve para sostener una serie de cajones o bandejas suspendidas y abiertas, fabricadas en madera de roble.

Se si guarda all'opprimente panorama industriale del terminale navale di Tsing Yi's, questo appartamento a Villa Esplanda risulta minuscolo. La giovane coppia di sposi proprietaria dell'appartamento diede il via a un programma di ristrutturazione pur avendo a disposizione un budget limitato. Sun Wong della Sunaqua Concept iniziò la progettazione tenendo conto di quelli che erano gli hobby dei proprietari; essi possedevano una vasta collezione di libri e di giochi elettronici. L'intenzione era quella di rispecchiare il carattere dei proprietari creando comfort e intimità con le cose di cui si circondavano volentieri. Il primo obiettivo è stato quindi quello di progettare un sistema di scaffalature e vetrine a misura per queste collezioni. Ne è risultata una scaffalatura continua lungo tutta la parete e il soffitto tra zona pasti e soggiorno. La struttura composita di acciaio grezzo sostiene una serie di casse aperte e travi sospese di legno di quercia.

9 tubo house

The functionality and beauty of a 50-year-old model for space-making is resurrected in this «minimum residence».

casa 9 tubo

La funcionalidad y la belleza de un modelo de hace cincuenta años para crear espacios resucita en esta «residencia mínima».

casa 9 tubo

La funzionalità e la bellezza di un modello di space-making vecchio di 50 anni, viene fatta resuscitare in questa «abitazione minima».

PROJECT LOCATION **MITAKA, TOKYO**
ARCHITECT / DESIGNER **MAKOTO KOIZUMI**
PHOTOGRAPHER **SOICHI MURAZUMI**
TEXT **REIKO KASAI & TATSUO ISO**

9 Tubo House is the house that interior designer Akoto Koizumi reconstructed on the basis of the 1957 house by the late architect Mr. Makoto Masuzawa. The original house was famous for making a small area comfortable. In a 1999 exhibition, when the structure model of a «minimum residence» was reproduced, the curator, Shu Hagiwara, asked Mr. Koizumi to re-design, and convert his own mansion based on this concept, for the exhibition. Many people were attracted to its functionality and beauty, and started requesting the same design. Producer Ysuyuki Okazaki commercialised «9 Tubo House», and created an industry based on this concept.

La 9 Tubo es la casa que el diseñador de interiores Akoto Koizumi reconstruyó basándose en la casa de 1957, del difunto arquitecto Makoto Masuzawa. La casa original fue famosa por lograr hacer confortable un pequeño espacio. En una exposición de 1999, cuando se reprodujo el modelo de estructura de «residencia mínima», el comisario, Shu Hagiwara, pidió a Koizumi que rediseñara y convirtiera para la exposición su vieja mansión, inspirándose en este concepto. Muchas personas se sintieron atraídas por su funcionalidad y belleza, y empezaron a encargar el mismo diseño. El productor Ysuyuki Okazaki comercializó la «casa 9 Tubo», y creó toda una industria basada en este concepto.

9 tubo house è la casa che l'architetto di interni Akoto Koizumi ha ricostruito sulla base di un casa del 1957 del defunto architetto sig. Makoto Masuzawa. La vecchia abitazione era famosa perché pur essendo piccola era molto confortevole. Durante una mostra nel 1999 che presentava modelli per «abitazioni minime», il curatore, Shu Agiwara, chiese al sig. Koizumi di riprogettare e trasformare, per la mostra stessa, la sua propria abitazione in base a questo concetto. Diverse persone di dimostrarono affascinate dalla sua bellezza e funzionalità e cominciarono a desiderare lo stesso per le proprie abitazioni. Il produttore Ysuyuki Okazaki ha commercializzato il progetto della 9 tubo house e ne ha creato una vera e propria industria.

beaver house

On a tiny site with soft ground, the designers of this house have both burrowed underground and reached for the sky.

casa beaver

En un diminuto solar en una zona de terreno blando, los diseñadores de esta casa han optado, por una parte, por excavar bajo el terreno, mientras por otro tratan de rozar el cielo.

casa beaver

Su un terreno minuscolo con suolo morbido, i due designer di questa casa hanno scavato nel sottosuolo per cercare di raggiungere il cielo.

PROJECT LOCATION **KOTO-KU, TOKYO**
TYPE **HOUSE**
ARCHITECT / DESIGNER **AKIRA YONEDA & MASAHIRO KIEDA**
PHOTOGRAPHER **KOJI OKUMURA**
TEXT **REIKO KASAI & TATSUO ISO**

This is a small residence on a site near the Ara Rive was created by Akira Yoneda and designer Masahiro Ikeda. A high artificial riverbank obstructs a direct view to the river from nearby locations. Therefore, the client requested that the house should be constructed as high as possible so that views could be afforded from upstairs. The building was extended to the maximum limit and resembles floating ship on soft ground. The first floor, containing living and dining room, is below ground level. Although there are no windows, it takes in plenty of natural light through skylights lights that are mounted along the ceiling edge. An open staircaise rises upward and leads to the master bedroom, which is projected outwards as if floating from the building. A spiral staircase leads inot the childrens room. The roof, which can be reached from the third-floor balcony, is higher than the riverbank and offers a great view of the river.

Esta pequeña residencia situada en un solar cercano al río Ara fue concebida por Akira Yoneda y el diseñador Masahiro Ikeda. Una elevada ribera artificial impide una vista directa del río desde los lugares cercanos. Por lo tanto, el cliente pidió que la casa se construyera lo más alto posible para lograr tener vistas desde la planta de arriba. El edificio se extendió hasta el límite máximo y se asemeja a un barco flotante sobre el terreno blando. La primera planta, en la que están ubicados la sala de estar y el comedor, está construida por debajo del nivel del terreno. Aunque no hay ventanas, entra abundante luz natural a través de los tragaluces montados a lo largo del borde del techo. Por unas escaleras abiertas que suben a la planta de arriba se accede al dormitorio principal, que está proyectado hacia fuera, como si flotara aparte del edificio. Una escalera en espiral conduce a la habitación de los niños. El tejado, al que puede accederse desde el balcón de la tercera planta, está más elevado que la ribera y ofrece una espléndida vista del río.

Questa piccola residenza su un terreno vicino Ara Rive è stata creata da Akira Yoneda e Masahiro Ikeda. Un'alta sponda artificiale del fiume ne ostruiva la vista diretta se lo si guardava da posizioni vicine. Per questo il cliente desiderava che la casa fosse costruita il più alta possibile, così da permettere la visuale sul fiume dal piano superiore. La casa è stata ampliata il più possibile e assomiglia ad una nave galleggiante su terreno morbido. Il primo piano in cui si trovano salotto e sala da pranzo è sotto il livello del terreno. Nonostante ciò non ci sono finestre e la luce naturale entra in abbondanza da lucernari posti lungo i lati del soffitto. Una scala aperta porta alla camera da letto principale, costruita all'esterno, come se galleggiasse a fianco all'edificio. Una scala a chiocciola porta alla camera dei bambini. Il tetto che si può raggiungere dal balcone del terzo piano, è più alto della sponda del fiume e ne offre una vista spettacolare.

borzoi house

This courtyard house has a rather futuristic design.

casa borzoi

Esta casa con jardín interior tiene un diseño algo futurista.

casa borzoi

Questa casa con cortile interno ha un design alquanto futuristico.

PROJECT LOCATION **CHIBA PREFECTURE, JAPAN**
FLOOR AREA **933 SQFT / 87 SQM**
ARCHITECT / DESIGNER **NORISADA MAEDA / N MAEDA ATELIER**
PHOTOGRAPHER **HIROSHI SHINOZAWA**
TEXT **KWAH MENG CHING**

This courtyard house is unique and eye-catching. The most striking point about this timber and steel structured house is undoubtedly its form. Lying on a low plinth is a form of an elongated elliptical cross section, with a radius of curvature that is different at both ends. The metallic exterior skin that shines and glistens under the sun further renders the house a futuristic quality that distinguishes it from its neighbours. Yet, this seemingly closed form with no apparent windows to the exterior speaks a different story once its exterior wall is conqueed. The entrance foyer is in a courtyard garden. A curved wall on one side sets the tone for the remaining parts of the house. The three internal courtyard gardens give the inward-looking house an openness that is otherwise unsuspected from the outside.

Esta casa con jardín interior es única y llamativa. Lo que más llama la atención en esta casa con una estructura de madera y acero es, sin duda, su forma. Construida sobre un zócalo bajo, su forma consta de una sección transversal elíptica alargada, con un radio de curvatura que difiere en cada uno de los extremos. El revestimiento exterior metálico, que brilla y refulge bajo el sol, le da además a la casa un carácter futurista que la distingue de las edificaciones vecinas. Sin embargo, esta forma aparentemente cerrada, en la que no se advierten ventanas al exterior, es totalmente diferente nada más atravesar su muro exterior. El vestíbulo de entrada está en un jardín interior. Un muro curvo en uno de los lados marca la pauta en las otras partes de la casa. Los tres jardines interiores proporcionan a esta introvertida casa una amplitud que no se sospechaba desde el exterior.

Questa casa con cortile interno è appariscente e unica nel suo genere. L'aspetto più singolare di questa costruzione in legno e acciaio è senza dubbio la sua forma. Posta su un basso zoccolo, ha la forma di una sezione obliqua di un'ellissi allungata con raggio diverso ai due poli. La copertura metallica esterna che splende e scintilla al sole, dona alla casa un aspetto futuristico oltre che distinguerla tra quelle del vicinato. Inoltre, questa forma esteriore chiusa, senza finestre visibili all'esterno, si trasforma completamente una volta oltrepassato il suo muro esterno. L'atrio di ingresso si trova in un cortile interno. Una parete curva da una parte dell'ingresso dà già un assaggio dello stile del resto della casa. I tre giardini interni regalano alla casa un'ariosità altrimenti insospettabile dall'esterno.

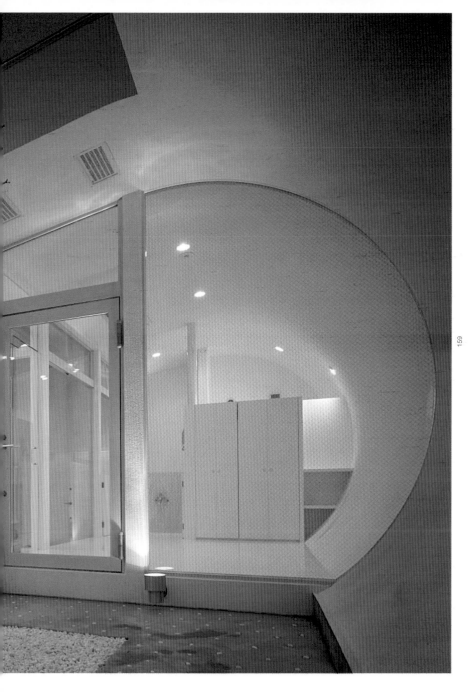

c house

This house on a small site has two floors of commercial restaurant space wrapped around a private living core in the configuration of a letter C.

casa c

Esta casa, construida sobre un pequeño solar, tiene dos plantas destinadas para uso comercial, en concreto a un restaurante, que envuelven un núcleo residencial privado con forma de letra C.

casa c

Questa casa edificata su un'area ristretta, ospita su due piani un ristorante che circonda in un abbraccio, come appunto una lettera c, un cuore costituito da un'abitazione privata.

PROJECT LOCATION TOKYO, JAPAN
FLOOR AREA 1227 SQFT / 114 SQM
ARCHITECT/DESIGNER TOSHIMITSU KUNO, NOBUYUKI NOMURA, TELE-DESIGN COLLABORATIVE NETWORK
PHOTOGRAPHER TATSUYA NOAKI
TEXT KWAH MENG CHING

Located at the junction where five roads intersect, C House is different from the inconspicuous faceless buildings in the surrounding urban fabric. This difference is manifested in both the architectural treatment of the volume and the usage programme. The building has two basements and two stories. The structure – part steel frame, part reinforced concrete – is being used as both a private residence and a restaurant. This definition of the public/private relationship in urban living attempts to steer away from the distinct duality of public and private and moves towards a more encompassing approach where the private living space is 'wrapped' by the public commercial space. The distinct boundary between public and private is thus diluted, transgressed and shared.

Ubicada en un cruce en el que confluyen cinco vías urbanas, la Casa C difiere de las discretas edificaciones despersonalizadas del tejido urbano circundante. La diferencia radica tanto en el tratamiento arquitectónico del volumen como en el uso que se le da al edificio. La casa tiene dos sótanos y dos plantas. La estructura – en parte de acero, en parte de hormigón armado – se utiliza a la vez de residencia privada y de restaurante. Esta definición de la relación entre lo público y lo privado en la vida urbana intenta distanciarse de la marcada dualidad de lo público y lo privado y se dirige hacia un enfoque más global, en el que el espacio residencial privado queda 'envuelto' por el espacio público de uso comercial. De esta forma, la nítida frontera entre lo público y lo privado se diluye, se sobrepasa y se comparte.

Situata all'incrocio di cinque diverse strade, la casa c si differenzia dalle costruzioni poco appariscenti e senza carattere del tessuto edilizio che la circonda. La differenza è chiara sia nella cura architettonica del volume che nello scopo stesso per cui è stata progettata. La costruzione ha due diverse fondamenta e due diverse storie. La struttura, in parte uno scheletro in acciaio e in parte cemento armato, viene usata sia come abitazione privata che come ristorante. Questo tipo di visione della relazione tra pubblico e privato vuol far dimenticare la netta dualità tra le due sfere e invita ad un approccio più globalizzante, in cui gli spazi privati vengono 'abbracciati' da quelli pubblici. Il confine netto tra pubblico e privato viene così ammorbidito, oltrepassato e condiviso.

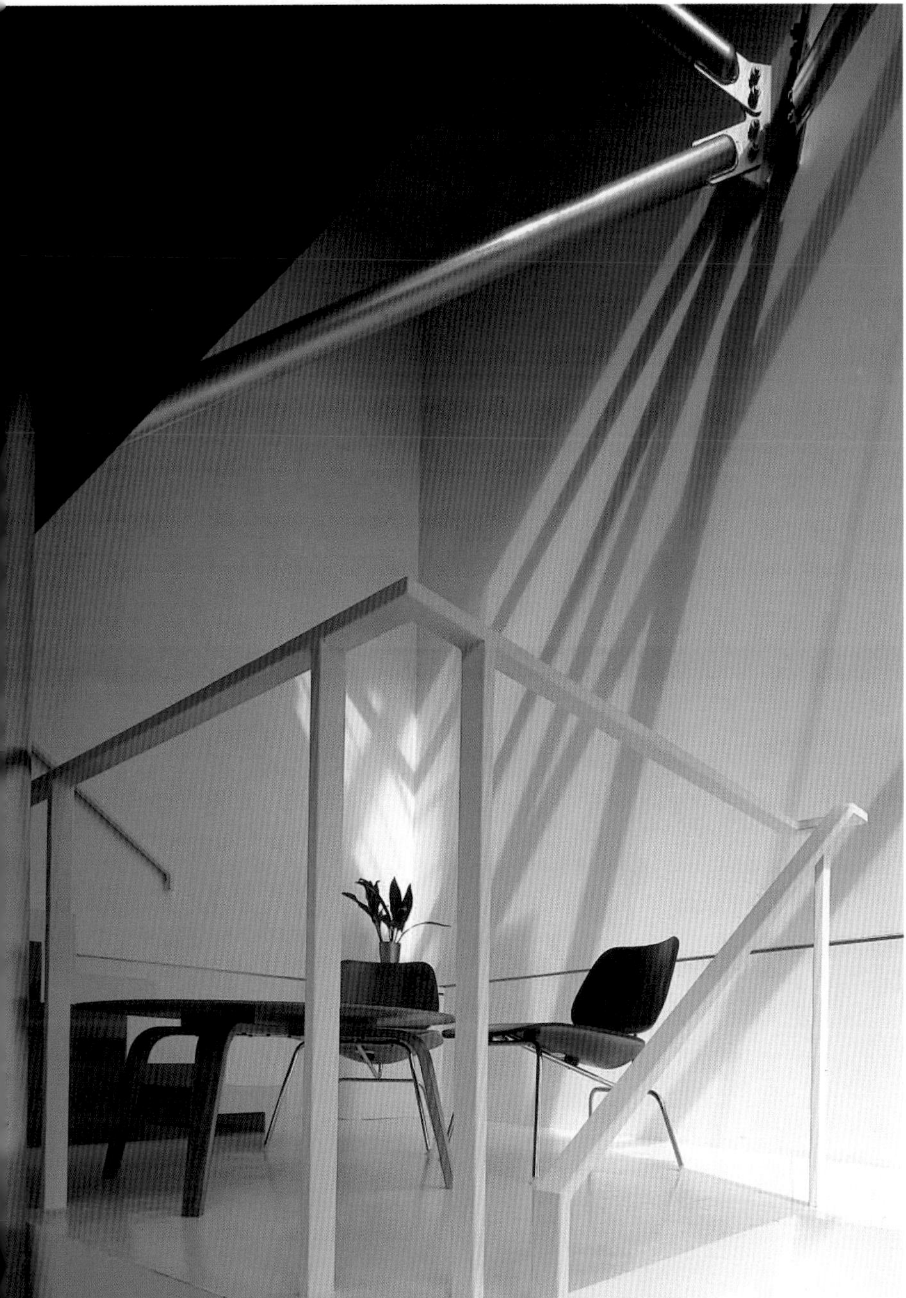

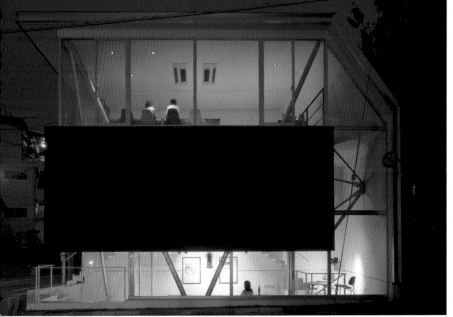

hachijo atelier

The Hachijo Atelier is an inquiry into the concept of «architecture as landscape».

estudio en hachijo

En este estudio de Hachijo se lleva a cabo un ensayo del concepto de «arquitectura como paisaje».

atelier hachijo

L' atelier hachijo è un'indagine vera e propria nell'ambito del concetto di «architettura quale paesaggio».

PROJECT LOCATION **HACHIJO ISLAND, TOKYO, JAPAN**
ARCHITECT / DESIGNER **NORIHIKO DAN / NORIHIKO DAN AND ASSOCIATES**
PHOTOGRAPHER **MITSUMASA FUJITSUKA**
TEXT **KWAH MENG CHENG**

Surrounded by a verdant tropical landscape, the Hachijo Atelier sits on a westward-facing slope overlooking picturesque black cliffs by the Pacific Ocean. This is a vacation home and studio for the architect's father, who is a composer and author, with an exterior performance space for Taiko drumming. The dual role of the house, being both a private retreat and an open-air theatre at the same time, necessitates a careful balance between enclosure and openness. The private functions of two bedrooms, atelier and the wet areas are arranged on the 'bowstring' side with fenestration fronting the view. The public living room in the house opens up towards the south and fronts the outdoor terrace. In the Hachijo Atelier, the two outdoor terraces are as much a part of the 'interior' of the house as the rest of the spaces are. These flag-stoned terraces fan out to the south and provide a natural extension of the interior living spaces.

Rodeado por un verde paisaje tropical, el estudio de Hachijo está situado en una ladera occidental, con vistas a los pintorescos acantilados negros junto al océano Pacífico. Esta construcción le sirve de casa de recreo y de estudio al padre del arquitecto, que es compositor y escritor, y cuenta con un espacio en el exterior destinado a conciertos con tambores Taiko. La doble función de la casa, que sirve a un tiempo de retiro privado y de teatro al aire libre, exige un cuidado equilibrio entre los espacios cerrados y los abiertos. Las funciones privadas de los dos dormitorios, el estudio y las zonas húmedas están dispuestas por el 'lado de la cuerda', donde la superficie acristalada enmarca las vistas en un primer plano. La sala de estar pública en el interior de la casa se abre hacia el sur y da a la terraza exterior. En este estudio en la isla de Hachijo, las dos terrazas exteriores están tan integradas en el 'interior' de la casa como el resto de los espacios. Estas terrazas enlosadas se abren en abanico hacia el sur y hacen de extensión natural de los espacios interiores.

Circondato da un verdeggiante paesaggio tropicale l'atelier hachijo è situato su un declivio rivolto a ovest che domina dall'alto le pittoresche scogliere nere del Pacifico. Funge sia da casa per le vacanze che da studio per il padre dell'architetto, compositore e autore, con un palco esterno per suonare i tamburi Taiko. Il doppio ruolo della casa, rifugio privato e teatro open air, esigeva un'attenta opera di bilanciamento tra i pieni e i vuoti. Le zone private, due camere da letto, l'atelier, il bagno, sono poste sul lato a 'corda d'arco' con grandi vetrate che offrono uno splendido panorama. Il salotto pubblico si apre verso il lato sud e guarda verso la terrazza all'esterno. Nell'atelier hachijo le due terrazze esterne fanno più parte dell'interno di quanto non faccia il resto della casa. Queste terrazze in pietra si aprono verso il sud e costituiscono un prolungamento naturale dell'interno della casa.

house at matsubara

A careful composition of folding planes and fenestrations have created a house that has a natural air-condition.

casa en matsubara

Con una esmerada composición de planos y ventanas que se combinan entre sí se ha creado una casa con aire acondicionado natural.

casa a matsubara

Un'attenta composizione di piani inclinati, porte e finestre, ha creato una casa fornita di aria condizionata naturale.

PROJECT LOCATION **SETAGAYA-KU, JAPAN**
ARCHITECT / DESIGNER **SATOSHI OKADA**
PHOTOGRAPHER **HIROYUKI HIRAI**
TEXT **REIKO KASAI & TATSUO ISO**

This sparsely filled, rectangular shaped residence emphasises volumes and planes. It has two skins that wrap and fold to carve out exterior courtyards and the interior spaces of the home. The perimeter wall uses lightweight reinforced concrete for the first and second floor, while unit slabs of lightweight steel frame are used for the roof. The living, dining rooms, and a kitchen are on the second floor. The bedroom, tearoom, bathroom and toilet are on the first floor.

En esta residencia de forma rectangular y con amplios espacios semivacíos resaltan los volúmenes y los planos. Tiene dos revestimientos que se envuelven y combinan entre sí para conformar los patios exteriores y los espacios interiores de la vivienda. En el muro que cerca el recinto se emplea hormigón armado ligero para la primera y la segunda planta, mientras que para el tejado se utilizan placas de una estructura metálica ligera. La sala de estar, el comedor y la cocina se encuentran en la segunda planta; el dormitorio, el salón de té, el cuarto de baño y el tocador, en la primera.

Questa residenza rettangolare poco arredata, mette in risalto i piani e i volumi. Ha due rivestimenti che la avvolgono e si piegano a creare un cortile esterno e uno spazio abitativo interno. La parete perimetrale è di cemento armato leggero nei due primi piani, mentre singole lastre di acciaio leggero sono utilizzate per il tetto. Soggiorno, sala da pranzo e una cucina si trovano al secondo piano. Camera da letto, tearoom, bagno e bagno di servizio sono al primo piano.

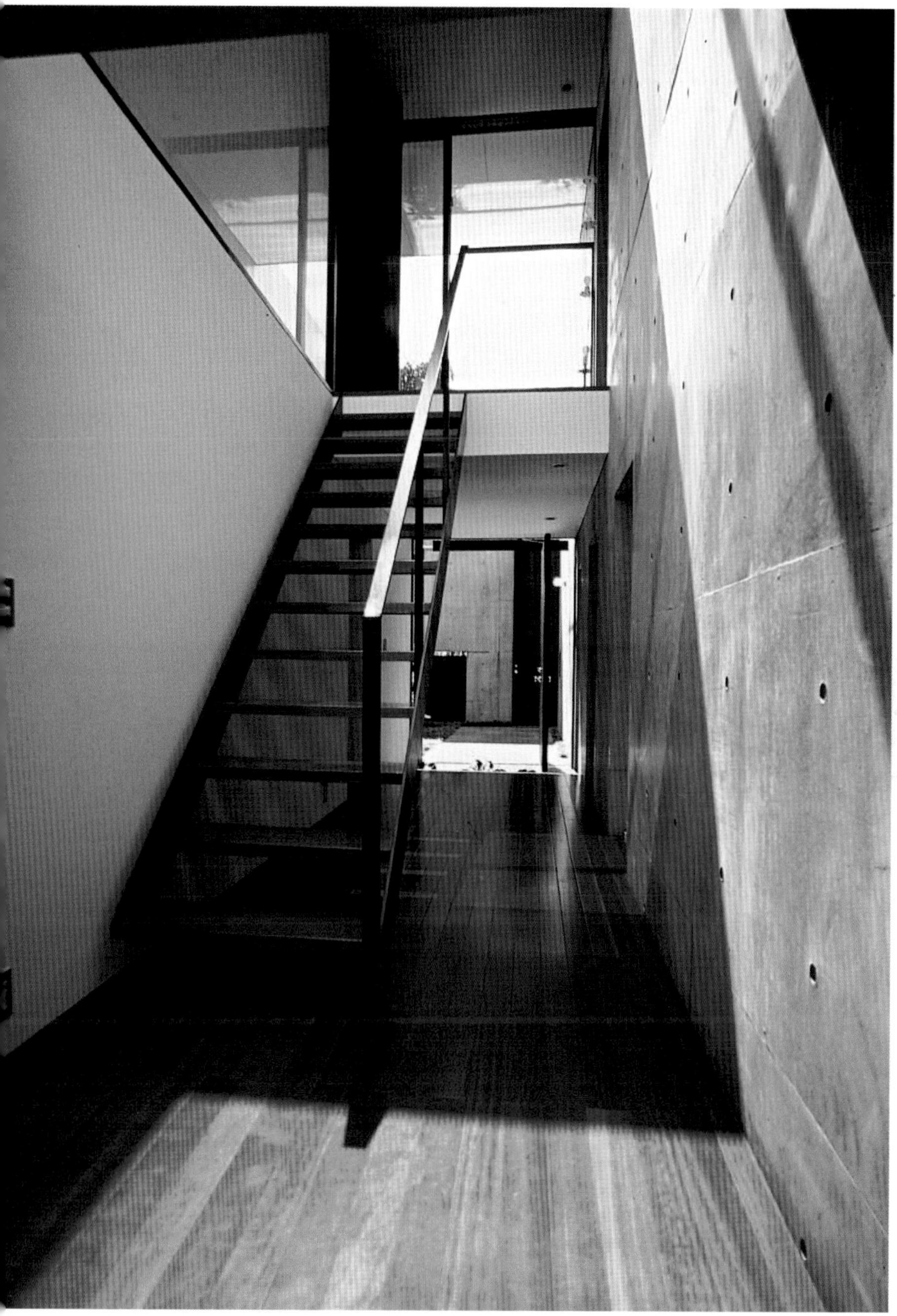

house at mount fuji

An appreciation for a stunning natural landscape have given this house on the foothills of Mount Fuji a perfect harmony with its surroundings.

casa en el monte fuji

Esta casa en las estribaciones del Monte Fujimori refleja el deslumbrante paisaje natural en armonía perfecta con su entorno.

casa sul monte fuji

L'amore per un paesaggio naturale meraviglioso ha regalato a questa casa ai piedi del monte Fuji un aspetto che si armonizza perfettamente con ciò che la circonda.

PROJECT LOCATION YAMANASHI PREFECTURE, JAPAN
ARCHITECT / DESIGNER SATOSHI OKADA / SATOSHI OKADA ARCHITECTS
PHOTOGRAPHER HIROYUKI HIRAI
TEXT KWAH MENNG CHING

Situated 1200m above sea-level among a tree plantation in the northern foothills of Mt. Fuji is this weekend villa. On the gently inclined site are a number of deciduous trees and a forest of white birch towards the north. The client wanted to build a small house to appreciate the tranquil surrounding nature. A diagonally folded wall divides the house into two realms – one is a big living space and the other contains bedrooms and a bathroom. The ceiling height in the living gradually changes from 3.8m to 5.3m in accordance with the sloping roof. As a contrast, the dining and kitchen are compressed beneath the loft as a space with 2m heigh ceiling. The progression through the house is spatially dramatic, and induces an appreciation of the surrounding nature.

A 1.200 m sobre el nivel del mar, entre una plantación de árboles en las estribaciones septentrionales del Monte Fuji, se levanta esta casa de recreo. Hacia el norte, en un terreno suavemente inclinado, hay una serie de árboles de hoja caduca y un bosque de abedules. El cliente deseaba construir una casa pequeña para apreciar el tranquilo entorno natural. Un muro en diagonal divide la casa en dos ámbitos: uno está constituido por una gran sala de estar, y el otro consta de los dormitorios y un cuarto de baño. La altura del techo en la sala de estar varía gradualmente de 3,8 m a 5,3 m de acuerdo con la inclinación del tejado. Como contraste, el comedor y la cocina se comprimen bajo el desván, logrando un espacio con un techo de 2 m de alto. Según avanzamos por la casa, sentimos con fuerza la presencia del espacio y se pone de relieve la naturaleza del entorno.

Questa villa per i fine settimana è situata a 1200 metri sul livello del mare, in mezzo a un bosco nelle colline a nord, ai piedi del monte Fuji. Su questo dolce pendio ci sono diversi alberi decidui e un bosco di betulle bianche rivolto a nord. Il cliente desiderava costruire una piccola casa per godere del tranquillo ambiente naturale. Una parete piegata diagonalmente divide la casa in due zone, una con un grande soggiorno e l'altra con camere da letto e bagno. L'altezza del soffitto nel soggiorno cambia gradualmente da 3.8 m a 5.3 m in armonia con l'inclinazione del tetto. La sala da pranzo e la cucina invece sono come compresse sotto il solaio con il loro soffitto alto solo 2 m. La progressione spaziale attraverso la casa è, per così dire, drammatica e invita ad apprezzare la natura circostante.

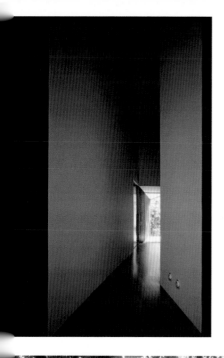

k house lounge

Despite a small floor area, the renovation of the second storey of this house proposes a space for a new independent urban lifestyle.

casa salón k

A pesar de la escasa superficie habitable, la reforma de la segunda planta de esta casa propone un espacio para un nuevo estilo de vida urbana independiente.

casa-salotto k

Pur se costruita su un area ristretta, la ristrutturazione del secondo piano di questa casa ha creato spazio sufficiente per godere un nuovo stile di vita urbano.

PROJECT LOCATION **CENTRAL TOKYO, JAPAN**
FLOOR AREA **484 SQFT / 45 SQM**
ARCHITECT / DESIGNER **HIROYUKI MATSUSHIMA / D.M.A.**
PHOTOGRAPHER **D.M.A.**
TEXT **KWAH MENG CHING**

For Hiroyuki Matsushima of DMA, it has become increasingly difficult to create a dwelling space within the contemporary urban environment by relying on former architectural ideologies. This is so because the traditional rituals of dining and living within a house are more regularly being carried out in the urban landscape. The city, with its extensive network of restaurants, café and convenience stores, is like the living room, dining and kitchen for the urban dweller. Matsushima feels that since domestic functions have infiltrated out into the urban scape, the original living and dining rooms should not be a closed internal environment. Instead, they should open out, extend to and connect with the urban expanse.

Para Hiroyuki Matsushima de DMA se ha vuelto cada vez más difícil crear un espacio residencial dentro del entorno urbano contemporáneo basándose en las antiguas tendencias arquitectónicas. Esto es así porque los tradicionales rituales de comer y vivir dentro de una casa se trasladan cada vez más al entorno urbano. La ciudad, con su amplia red de restaurantes, cafés y supermercados de barrio, es como la sala de estar, el comedor y la cocina para sus habitantes. Matsushima es de la opinión de que, dado que las funciones domésticas se han infiltrado en el espacio urbano, la sala de estar y el comedor originarios no deberían ser un ambiente interior cerrado; por el contrario, deberían abrirse, extenderse y conectarse al entorno urbano.

Per Hiroyuki Matsushima della DMA era diventato sempre più difficile creare uno spazio abitativo nel tessuto urbano moderno, facendo affidamento sulle direttive canoniche dell'architettura. E questo perché quelli che una volta erano rituali tradizionali da svolgersi in casa, quali i pasti e lo stare assieme, si sono spostati sempre più all'esterno, nel paesaggio urbano. La città con la sua vasta rete di ristoranti, bar, negozi, si è trasformata nel soggiorno, nella sala da pranzo, nella cucina del cittadino moderno. Matsushina ritiene che dal momento in cui le esigenze domestiche si sono spostate in città, i soggiorni e le sale da pranzo non dovrebbero più starsene chiusi all'interno. Al contrario, essi dovrebbero essere aperti, allungati verso lo spazio urbano ed uniti ad esso.

m house

A long, narrow living area is made spacious
and airy by a triple-height internal void space.

casa m

Una vivienda larga y estrecha se vuelve espaciosa y
aireada gracias a un espacio interior vacío de triple altura.

casa m

Un'area abitativa lunga e stretta è resa spaziosa ed arieggiata
grazie ad un sistema a tripla altezza di spazi interni vuoti.

PROJECT LOCATION SETAGAYA-KU, TOKYO
ARCHITECT / DESIGNER EISHIN MATSUNAGA @ CLIP
PHOTOGRAPHER CLIP
TEXT REIKO KASAI & TATSUO ISO

The M House is located in a densely packed residential neighbourhood in Tokyo. It contains three floors that are configured about a triple height internal void. The house is divided into two zones: a formal or public western area, incorporating the triple height void, and an informal or private eastern area, enclosing the bedroom, stairs and storage area.

La Casa M se encuentra en un barrio residencial de Tokio con una elevada densidad de población. Consta de tres plantas, configuradas en torno a un espacio interior vacío de triple altura. La casa está dividida en dos partes: una zona occidental formal o pública, que comprende el espacio vacío de triple altura, y una zona oriental de carácter informal o privado, en la que se encuentran el dormitorio, unas escaleras y un espacio para guardar cosas.

La casa m è situata in un quartiere densamente popolato di Tokyo. E' composta da tre «mezzi piani» consistenti in spazi interni vuoti a tre altezze. La casa è divisa in due zone: una zona a ovest pubblica e formale con i tre mezzi piani vuoti, e una zona privata a est in cui si trovano la camera da letto, le scale e il ripostiglio.

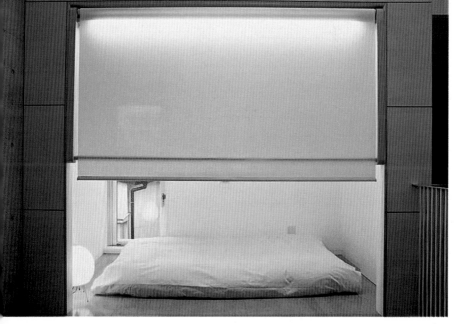

natural illuminance

This house may be small and inward-looking, but its white box is filled with light and air that enriches the soul.

iluminación natural

Esta casa puede que sea pequeña e «introvertida», pero su forma cúbica blanca está llena de luz y de aire, enriqueciendo el espíritu.

illuminazione naturale

Questa casa può sembrare piccola e chiusa in sé, ma in realtà le sue mura bianche sono così sature di luce e aria, da essere un vero balsamo per l'anima.

PROJECT LOCATION **TOKYO, JAPAN**
FLOOR AREA **715 SQFT / 67 SQM**
ARCHITECT / DESIGNER **MASAKI ENDOH + MASAHIRO IKEDA (EDH ENDOH DESIGN HOUSE + MIAS)**
PHOTOGRAPHER **MASAKI ENDOH**
TEXT **KWAH MENG CHING**

This cubic building has a symmetrically composed wrap-around façade of white square panels with slit glass separating each of them. Being in a northern temperate climate, the sun rises from the east, stands in the south before setting in the west. The white wrapped-around façade has maximised this sun path and floods the interior with a smoothing brightness. The northern façade of the house has a different treatment with two structural columns painted in black. The wet areas are concentrated in one corner and finished with glass as far as possible to give an expansion of space. The main space within the house is the living-cum-dining, which occupies nearly one-third of the total house area.

Esta construcción cúbica tiene una fachada envolvente compuesta de forma simétrica, de paneles cuadrados blancos con franjas de cristal separándolos. Al estar en un clima septentrional templado, el sol sale por el este y pasa por el sur antes de ponerse por el oeste. La fachada envolvente blanca saca el máximo partido de este recorrido del sol e inunda el interior de un suave brillo. La fachada septentrional de la casa tiene un tratamiento distinto, con dos columnas estructurales pintadas de color negro. Los lugares húmedos se concentran en una de las esquinas y están terminadas en cristal, lo más lejos posible, para proporcionar una sensación de amplitud. La principal habitación de la casa es el salón-comedor, que ocupa casi un tercio de la superficie total de la vivienda.

Questa costruzione cubica è ricoperta simmetricamente in tutti i suoi lati da pannelli squadrati divisi gli uni dagli altri da vetro. Trovandosi in una zona a nord, dal clima temperato, il sole si leva a est, si alza a sud e cala a ovest. La facciata bianca ha tratto il massimo dal cammino del sole e inonda l'interno di una gradevole luminosità. La facciata a nord è stata pensata invece in modo diverso, con due colonne portanti nere. Il bagno e la cucina sono stretti in un angolo e rifiniti il più possibile con vetro, così da dare l'idea dell'espandersi dello spazio. La stanza più grande nella casa è il soggiorno-sala da pranzo che ne occupa un terzo dell'area totale.

oh house

This house for a family of three uses minimum means to achieve maximum effect.

casa oh

Esta casa, para una familia de tres personas, emplea los mínimos elementos posibles para lograr el máximo efecto.

oh house

Questa casa per una famiglia di tre persone raggiunge effetti massimi con mezzi minimi.

PROJECT LOCATION CHIBA PREFECTURE, JAPAN
FLOOR AREA **699 SQFT / 65 SQM**
ARCHITECT / DESIGNER **AKO NNAGAO / AKO NAGAO ARCHITECT OFFICE**
PHOTOGRAPHER **SATOSHI ASAKAWA**
TEXT **KWAH MENG CHING**

Hidden from public view, this house does not have the usual problem of how to maintain privacy within the public setting. On the contrary, the critical issue here lies in creating a house that is opened to the exterior. The result is a one-storey rectangular volume that capitalised on the longitudinal orientation of the site, creating a spacious garden on the southern front. The elevated floor of the house further renders it the illusion of floating in the garden.

Al quedar oculta de la vista pública, esta casa no presenta el problema habitual de cómo lograr intimidad dentro del espacio público. Por el contrario, aquí la cuestión fundamental es crear una casa que esté abierta al exterior. El resultado es un volumen rectangular de una sola planta que aprovecha la orientación longitudinal del solar, creando un espacioso jardín en la fachada sur. El piso elevado de la casa contribuye aún más a la ilusión de que está flotando en el jardín.

Nascosta alla vista, questa casa non deve affrontare il solito problema di dover mantenere la privacy in un ambiente pubblico. Al contrario, la questione più critica qui era creare proprio una casa che fosse aperta all'esterno. Il risultato è una costruzione rettangolare ad un unico piano che trae profitto dall'orientamento longitudinale con uno spazioso giardino sul fronte sud. Il piano leggermente elevato della casa, poi, gli dona l'impressione di galleggiare sul giardino.

rooftecture m

Shuhei Endo has created a home where the family can live together in a continuous strip of partially shared living space.

rooftecture m

Shuhei Endo ha creado una casa en la que la familia puede vivir junta en una franja continua de espacio residencial parcialmente compartido.

tetto m

Shuhei Endo ha creato una casa in cui la famiglia può vivere insieme sotto un nastro continuo di spazi abitativi parzialmente condivisi.

PROJECT LOCATION FUKUI PREFECTURE, JAPAN
ARCHITECT / DESIGNER SHHUHEI ENDO/SHUHEI ENDO ARCHITECT INSTITUTE
PHOTOGRAPHER YOSHIHARU MATSUMURA
TEXT KWAH MENG CHING

Rooftecture M is a house-cum-atelier sitting on a rectangular site. It has a small front with longitudinal sides. The client had requested the inclusion of an atelier where he can entertain visitors, with the more private family spaces as inconspicuous to the visitors as possible. Shuhei Endo proposed a solution whereby the different functional spaces are sheltered under a huge piece of bent corrugated metal sheet, acting as both the roof and walls on both longitudinal sides. This piece of metal is cut at a few locations in order to let in air and light.

La Rooftecture M es una casa-estudio construida sobre un solar rectangular. Tiene una pequeña fachada delantera de lados longitudinales. El cliente había encargado que se incluyera un estudio para poder recibir a las visitas, de forma que los espacios familiares más privados pasaran tan inadvertidos como fuera posible a los visitantes. Shuhei Endo propuso una solución en la que los distintos espacios funcionales estuvieran albergados bajo una enorme chapa de metal ondulada formando una curva, que sirve a un tiempo de tejado y de muros para ambos lados longitudinales. Este trozo de metal está cortado en algunos puntos para dejar entrar el aire y la luz.

Tetto m è una casa-atelier situata su un terreno rettangolare. Ha un fronte stretto e lati lunghi. Il cliente desiderava avere anche un atelier in cui ricevere gli ospiti, accanto agli spazi più privati che non dovevano però essere notati dagli estranei. Shuhei Endo propone una soluzione secondo la quale i diversi spazi vengono coperti da un enorme foglio di lamiera ondulata piegato con la funzione sia di tetto che di pareti per tutti e due i lati lunghi. In alcuni punti ci sono delle fessure che consentono il passaggio dell'aria e della luce.

screen house at senkawa

The problem of a tiny floor area has been transformed into an attractive architectural solution.

casa con mampara en senkawa

El problema de una minúscula superficie habitable se ha transformado en una atractiva solución arquitectónica.

casa con schermo a senkawa

Il problema di un'area abitativa piccolissima è stato trasformato con una soluzione architettonica veramente interessante.

PROJECT LOCATION **TOSHIMA-KU, TOKYO**
FLOOR AREA **1291 SQFT / 120 SQM**
ARCHITECT / DESIGNER **MIKIO TAI / ARCHITECT CAFE**
PHOTOGRAPHER **KATSUHISA KIDA**
TEXT **TEIKO KASAI**

This is a house of extremely small size. The architect thus had to devise some clever strategies for planning in a tight space. In order to save space, the stairs were installed outside the main building enclosed by a screen that can be opened and closed. The owners can change the opening-and-closing state and position of the screen freely according to their preferences. The top floor space is covered by lumber. This creates an interesting ribbed ceiling, which successfully brings the aesthetic of the external screen to the interior. The screen creates an attractive and delicate filtration of light both during the day and night.

Esta es una casa de tamaño sumamente reducido. Por esa razón, el arquitecto tuvo que concebir una serie de ingeniosas estrategias para realizar el diseño en un espacio tan limitado. Para ahorrar espacio, las escaleras se instalaron en el exterior del edificio principal, rodeadas por una mampara que se puede abrir y cerrar. Los inquilinos pueden variar a su gusto el estado de apertura y cierre y la posición de la mampara, según sus preferencias. El espacio del piso superior está cubierto de madera. De esta forma se crea un interesante techo estriado, que logra aportar al interior la estética de la mampara exterior. La mampara permite una atractiva y delicada filtración de la luz tanto de día como de noche.

Questa è una casa estremamente piccola. L'architetto ha di conseguenza dovuto usare tutta la sua fantasia per escogitare soluzioni appropriate a pianificare su uno spazio così ristretto. Per guadagnare spazio le scale sono state poste al di fuori dell'edificio principale, e sono protette da una specie di schermo in legno che può essere tenuto chiuso, ma che si può anche aprire. I proprietari possono decidere liberamente il grado di apertura di questo schermo e la sua posizione. Il piano più alto è coperto da travi di legno, cosa che crea un interessante soffitto rinforzato, che richiama con successo l'aspetto dello schermo esterno all'interno della casa. Lo schermo poi filtra in modo piacevole e delicato la luce sia durante il giorno che durante la notte.

studio yukobo

A charming ex-clinic building has been converted to a gallery for visiting artists.

estudio yukobo

Un precioso edificio de una antigua clínica ha sido transformado en una galería para artistas de visita.

studio yukobo

La bellissima costruzione che, una volta, ospitava una clinica è stata ora trasformata in una galleria d'arte.

PROJECT LOCATION CTOKYO, JAPAN
ARCHITECT / DESIGNER TOMOAKI TANAKA / FORMS
PHOTOGRAPHER FORMS
TEXT KWAH MENG CHING

This artist couple has started an organisation to support young artists, inviting them to stay at their residence and create work. Hence, they needed additional studio and gallery space, and also improved accommodation for themselves. So the project is composed of three elements: the addition to their existing wooden house, the transformation of a neighbouring 50-year-old ex-clinic building into a gallery space, and the insertion of a studio space for a sculptor. Tomoaki Tanaka of FORMS opted to reorganise the existing building resources instead of demolishing all and rebuilding.

Esta pareja de artistas ha fundado una organización de apoyo a jóvenes creadores, a los que invitan a alojarse en su residencia para que se dediquen a la creación artística. Por consiguiente, necesitaban espacio adicional para un estudio y una galería, además de un mayor espacio para ellos mismos. Así, el proyecto está compuesto por tres elementos: la unión de su antigua casa de madera, la transformación de un edificio de una clínica vecina de 50 años de antigüedad en una galería de arte y la inclusión de un estudio para un escultor. Tomoaki Tanaka de la agencia FORMS optó por reorganizar los recursos disponibles, en vez de demoler y reconstruir el edificio.

La coppia di artisti che ha commissionato il progetto, è a capo di un'associazione di appoggio per giovani artisti, che vengono spesso anche ospitati a vivere da loro per creare insieme opere d'arte. Per questo motivo si è reso necessario un nuovo studio, nonché una galleria, oltre ad un alloggio più comodo per se stessi. E' per questo che il progetto è composto da tre elementi: il prolungamento della casa in legno già esistente, la trasformazione di un edificio vecchio di 50 anni che ospitava una clinica in una galleria, e l'aggiunta di uno studio per uno scultore. Tomoaki Tanaka di FORMS ha scelto di riorganizzare l'edificio già esistente invece di abbatterlo e ricostruire tutto.

t-set house

The symbiotic dependency of two houses results in views, light and privacy.

conjunto t

La simbiótica dependencia de dos casas tiene como resultado vistas, luz y sensación de privacidad.

casa a t

La dipendenza simbiotica di due case ha avuto come risultato una visuale migliore, luce e privacy.

PROJECT LOCATION **TOKYO, JAPAN**
FLOOR AREA **614 SQFT / 57 SQM**
ARCHITECT / DESIGNER **MANABU CHIBA / CHIBBA MANABU ARCHITECTS**
PHOTOGRAPHER **NACASA & PARTNERS INC.**
TEXT **KWAH MENG CHING**

Manabu Chiba designs residential houses offer a great degree of porosity that engages the occupants with the cityscape, while not compromising privacy and comfort. T-set is a further development of his ideals and an attempt at urban design and planning, albeit on a small scale. The client bought a plot of land enough to build two independent detached houses. After studying the site, Chiba found that the most feasible way is to sub-divide the land into a L-plot and a rectangular plot. Together, the two rectangular plots of land form a 'T'. The T-set house sits on the L-shaped plot and is, like most houses in Tokyo, with its T-set small and compact.

Los diseños de casas residenciales de Manabu Chiba ofrecen un elevado grado de porosidad, que pone a los ocupantes en contacto con el paisaje urbano, sin sacrificar la sensación de privacidad ni el confort. El conjunto T supone un nuevo desarrollo de sus ideales constructivos y un intento de diseño y planificación urbanos, aunque a pequeña escala. El cliente compró una parcela de tierra suficiente para construir dos casas independientes, no adosadas. Tras estudiar el solar, Chiba llegó a la conclusión de que la opción más viable consistía en subdividir el terreno en dos parcelas, una en forma de L y otra rectangular. Juntas, las dos parcelas rectangulares forman una 'T'. La casa del conjunto T está construida sobre el solar en forma de L y es, como la mayoría de las casas de Tokio, pequeña y compacta, con su conjunto T.

Il design tipico di Manabu Chiba per case residenziali è caratterizzato da un elevato numero di aperture, tale che chi ci abita è totalmente immerso nel paesaggio urbano, pur mantenendo privacy e comfort. La casa a T rappresenta un ulteriore sviluppo di questo principio e un adeguamento alla progettazione e pianificazione urbana, seppur su scala ridotta. Il cliente aveva comprato un appezzamento di terreno grande abbastanza per costruirci due villette unifamiliari indipendenti. Dopo aver studiato il terreno, Chiba trovò che la soluzione migliore fosse quella di dividere il terreno in due, un lotto a L e uno rettangolare. Questi due lotti insieme formano una T. La casa a T è posta sul lotto a forma di L ed è, come quasi tutte le case di Tokyo, con la sua forma a T, piccola e compatta.

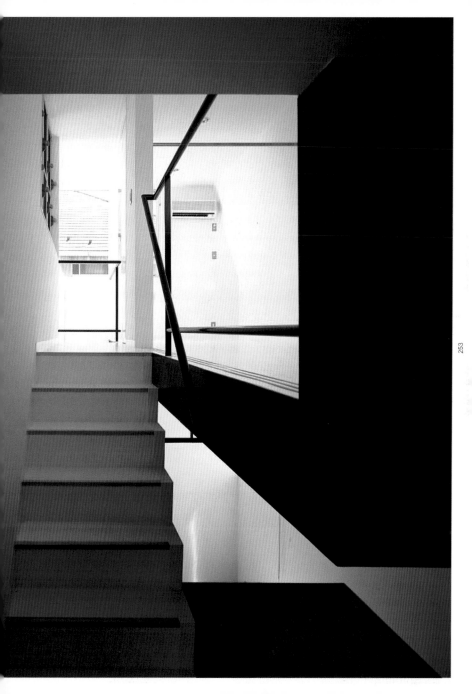

damansara perdana

Custom made furniture and Asian art adorn neutral surfaces in this apartment show unit.

damansara perdana

Los muebles, diseñados a la manera tradicional, y el arte asiático adornan las superficies neutras de este apartamento piloto.

damansara perdana

Mobilio tradizionale e arte asiatica regalano prestigio e aspetto unitario alle superfici neutre di questo appartamento.

PROJECT LOCATION **BANDAR DAMANSARA, MALAYSSIA**
ARCHITECT / DESIGNER **SUSANNE ZEIDLER, NG KIAN TECK / ZLG SDN BHD**
PHOTOGRAPHER **K. L NG**
TEXT **RICHARD SE**

The concept for this show unit was to use a contemporary approach with 'Asian' accents and highlights. Many of the display items selected by the client and the designers have been created by Asian artists, and were specifically chosen for this reason. They are composed and displayed throughout the show unit wherever suitable. The colour scheme is primarily composed of different hues of purple contrasting with different hues of grey. This was of great importance to the selection process of all the cushions, curtains, roman blinds, furniture and even the display items, which are all selected to complement each other.

El concepto para este apartamento piloto fue utilizar un enfoque contemporáneo con acentos y toques 'asiáticos'. Muchos de los elementos que aquí aparecen, seleccionados por el cliente y los diseñadores, han sido creados por artistas asiáticos y fueron elegidos precisamente por esta razón. Están distribuidos y expuestos por todo el apartamento de una forma acertada. El esquema de color se compone principalmente de diferentes tonos de púrpura que contrastan con los diferentes grises. Esto fue fundamental durante el proceso de selección de los cojines, cortinas, persianas romanas, muebles e incluso de los elementos decorativos, seleccionados para complementarse entre sí.

L'idea, finalizzata a dare aspetto omogeneo a questo appartamento, era quella di utilizzare, pur con approccio moderno, accenti e particolari asiatici. Molti degli articoli esibiti, scelti dal cliente e dagli architetti, sono stati creati da artisti asiatici, e proprio per questo trovano posto nell'appartamento. Sono disposti e messi in mostra ovunque in modo sempre adeguato. La paletta cromatica è composta principalmente da diversi toni di porpora che fanno da contrasto a diversi toni di grigio. A questo aspetto si è data la massima importanza quando si sono scelti i cuscini, le tende, le persiane, i mobili e appunto i soprammobili, complementari tutti l'un l'altro.

house at bukit antarabangsa

Alterations to an existing house have struck a balance between comfort, practicality and aesthetic value.

casa en bukit antarabangsa

Las reformas realizadas en esta casa ya existente han logrado el equilibrio entre la comodidad, el sentido práctico y el valor estético.

casa a bukit antarabangsa

Modifiche apportate ad una casa preesistente hanno portato ad un perfetto equilibrio tra comfort, praticità e pregi estetici.

PROJECT LOCATION **BUKIT ANTARABANGSA, MALAYSIA**
ARCHITECT / DESIGNER **RICHARD SE / PH+D DESIGN**
PHOTOGRAPHER **RICHARD SE**
TEXT **RICHARD SE**

The original house is one of the 120 units in a 12-year old estate designed by Malaysian architect Ken Yeang. It is a very simple concrete structure in a «Modern» style with two courtyards to take advantage of natural lighting and ventilation. One of the courtyards next to the kitchen had been roofed over by the previous residents. The client wanted to increase the living and dining areas. The designers opened up the view to the garden and hills where the dining and the living rooms are located. Existing brick walls were replaced with floor-to-ceiling glass doors for unobstructed views out to the rear. A small outdoor terrace was created at the adjoining space between the living and the dining room. It is a shelter with clear polycarbonate roof and a fine bamboo screen, converting this area into a breezy and shady space that is particularly enjoyable in the evenings. The living area and its terraces are now visually and physically extended into the garden and beyond.

La casa original es una de las 120 unidades de una urbanización de doce años de antigüedad diseñada por el arquitecto malayo Ken Yeang. Se trata de una estructura de hormigón muy sencilla en un estilo «moderno» con dos patios para aprovechar la luz y la ventilación naturales. El patio contiguo a la cocina fue techado por los propietarios anteriores. El cliente quería ampliar el salón y el comedor. Los diseñadores abrieron la vista al jardín y a las colinas desde el salón y el comedor. Las paredes de ladrillo que había fueron reemplazadas por puertas de cristal que van desde el suelo hasta el techo, para tener así una vista despejada de la parte trasera de la casa. Se hizo una pequeña terraza en el espacio que quedaba entre el salón y el comedor. Se trata de un refugio con un tejado de policarbonato claro y un fino biombo de bambú que convierten este área en un espacio fresco y sombreado, especialmente agradable por las tardes. Ahora, el salón y sus terrazas se extienden visual y físicamente hasta más allá del jardín.

La casa originale è una delle 120 progettate dall'architetto malesiano Ken 12 anni prima. E' una costruzione molto semplice e lineare in uno stile, per così dire, moderno, con due cortili che provvedono all'illuminazione naturale e all'aerazione. Uno dei cortili, vicino alla cucina, era stato coperto dagli inquilini precedenti. Il cliente desiderava ampliare la zona soggiorno e pranzo. Gli architetti hanno aperto la visuale in direzione del giardino e delle colline, dove appunto c'erano soggiorno e sala da pranzo. La preesistente parete in mattoni è stata sostituita da vetrate che arrivano fino al soffitto, e offrono una visuale libera fino in fondo. All'esterno, nello spazio attiguo, tra soggiorno e sala da pranzo, è stata costruita una piccola terrazza. Si tratta di un riparo con tetto in policarbonato trasparente e un parapetto in fine bamboo, che trasforma questa zona in uno spazio arieggiato e ombroso, da godersi particolarmente di sera. La zona soggiorno e le sue terrazze sono ora sia visivamente che, più propriamente, fisicamente prolungate fino nel giardino e oltre.

timber house at batu laut

This example of a house has the dining and living room as well as the private areas which are divided into three pavilions, in the open air.

casa de madera en batu laut

Este ejemplo de casa tiene el comedor, la sala de estar y las zonas privadas divididas en tres pabellones al aire libre.

casa in legno a batu laut

Questo è un esempio di casa che ospita soggiorno, sala da pranzo, oltre che le altre camere più private, in tre distinti padiglioni all'aperto.

PROJECT LOCATION **BATU LAUT, SELANGOR, MALAYSIA**
ARCHITECT/DESIGNER **C'ARCH ARCHITECTURE + DESIGN SDN BHD**
PHOTOGRAPHER **GERALD LOPEZ & AHMAD SABKI**
TEXT **RICHARD SE**

This house, with a strong tropical essence, consists of three separate but linked pavilions, requiring the occupants to physically exit the enclosures and re-enter to get into the different spaces. These are reminiscent of traditional Malaysian domestic architecture, with their mostly stilted timber structure, extensive openings and wide eaves and verandahs. The first pavillion contains the dining space and is surrounded by the garden. The living pavilion, which is opposite the dining pavilion, is raised and encompasses the formal entrance to the house. The third pavilion is detached from the public spaces and enjoys the intimacy of luxurious open baths set in private gardens.

Esta casa, con un carácter típicamente tropical, consta de tres pabellones separados pero conectados entre sí, lo que obliga a los habitantes a salir físicamente de los recintos para volver a entrar en los diferentes espacios. Esto son reminiscencias de la arquitectura doméstica tradicional de Malasia, con su estructura de madera, construida en su mayor parte sobre pilotes, sus grandes aberturas y los amplios aleros y terrazas. En el primer pabellón se encuentra el espacio destinado al comedor y está rodeado por el jardín. El pabellón de estar, situado enfrente del comedor, se alza sobre el suelo e incluye la entrada formal a la casa. El tercer pabellón está separado de los espacios públicos y goza de la intimidad de lujosos baños abiertos situados en los jardines privados.

Questa casa, dall'atmosfera fortemente tropicale, è costituita da tre padiglioni separati ma collegati tra loro. Per spostarsi da una stanza all'altra bisogna quindi uscire e rientrare da un padiglione all'altro attraverso corridoi. Sono reminiscenze della tradizionale architettura domestica malesiana, con le sue strutture per lo più a palafitte, porte e finestre molto ampie e larghi cornicioni e verande. Nel primo padiglione, circondato dal giardino, si trova la zona pranzo. Il padiglione con il soggiorno, di fronte a quello con la sala da pranzo, è rialzato e cinge l'entrata principale della casa. Il terzo padiglione è staccato dalle zone più pubbliche e gode dell'intimità di bagni lussuosi aperti, posti in giardini privati.

commonwealth avenue west

The designers at Wide Open Spaces have echoed their company name in the refurbishment.

commonwealth avenue west

Los diseñadores de Wide Open Spaces han hecho honor a su nombre en la renovación de casas.

commonwealth avenue west

I designer del Wide Open Space hanno voluto far riecheggiare il nome della loro società in questo restauro.

PROJECT LOCATION **COMMONWEALTH AVENUE WEST, SINGAPORE**
FLOOR AREA **1600 SQFT / 149 SQM**
ARCHITECT / DESIGNER **GAYLE LEONG AND DAPHNE ANG / WIDE OPEN SPACES**
PHOTOGRAPHER **KELLEY CHENG**
TEXT **NARELLE YABUKA**

The floor area of this apartment flat has been maximised with windows, a neutral treatment of floors and walls, and screens that allow visual penetration between rooms. A feeling of airiness has been created, with maximum light transmission into and through the interior by way of frosted glass doors. The variety of materials, that have been used, is modest. There is a cement screed floor in the living areas, the walls are painted in a pale fawn-brown, and dark timber architectural features divide and define spaces. Sparsely arranged, sculptural items of furniture, highlighted by halogen down-lights, join forces with the timber elements to punctuate the space.

La superficie habitable de este apartamento se ha ampliado al máximo con las ventanas, con el tratamiento neutro de los suelos y las paredes y con los biombos, que permiten un acceso visual a las habitaciones. Se ha conseguido una sensación de espaciosidad gracias a las puertas de cristal esmerilado, que posibilitan una intensa transmisión de luz no sólo hacia el interior, sino también a través de él. La variedad de materiales utilizados es moderada. En las zonas de estar, el suelo está recubierto de cemento, las paredes están pintadas de marrón-beige pálido y los rasgos arquitectónicos de la madera oscura dividen y definen los espacios. Los esculturales muebles, dispuestos de una forma dispersa y realzados por tenues luces halógenas, marcan, junto con los elementos de madera, el espacio.

Si è creata la sensazione di un ampliamento della superficie di questo appartamento grazie a finestre, al colore neutro di pavimenti e pareti, e a pannelli divisori che permettono di vedere da una stanza all'altra. L'impressione di ariosità, è data dalla luminosità trasmessa da porte in vetro satinato. Non è stata usata una gran varietà di materiali. Il pavimento della zona soggiorno è in cemento, le pareti sono marrone-fulvo pallido, e il mobilio in legno scuro divide e definisce gli spazi. Alcuni, ma non troppi pezzi d'arte, quali sculture, messi in risalto da lampade alogene con luce soffusa, contribuiscono, insieme all'arredamento in legno, a dare enfasi agli spazi.

figaro street house

Singaporean artist and designer Michael Cu Fua's house is testament to his design sensibilities for a modern tropical house – clean, simple and functional.

casa en figaro street

La casa del artista y diseñador Michael Cu Fua, nativo de Singapur, es un testimonio de su sensibilidad artística por la casa tropical moderna: pureza en el diseño, sencillez y funcionalidad.

casa a figaro street

La casa dell'artista nonché designer Michael Cu Fua's di Singapore rappresenta il suo testamento artistico con la sua predilezione per un design tropicale moderno, pulito, semplice e funzionale.

PROJECT LOCATION **FIGARO STREET, SINGAPORE**
FLOOR AREA **1500 SQFT / 140 SQM**
ARCHITECT / DESIGNER **MICHAEL CUFUA / CU FUA ASSOCIATES**
PHOTOGRAPHER **THE PRESS ROOM**
TEXT **NARELLE YABUKA**

Cu Fua engaged the services of his wife for the rennovation or their terrace house in Figaro Street. The result is a space that has the semi-unkempt charm of a male artist, moderated by female sensibility. A defining design element is the black floor: a monolithic base stretching from the front porch to the dining area. Another feature is the enclosure, or lack thereof, of the bedroom. It opens unabashedly into the living room, enclosed only by sliding glass partitions and curtains. However, such a lack of visual segregation was not an exercise in voyeurism; the intention was to alleviate claustrophobic spatial restrictions.

Cu Fua contrató los servicios de su mujer para la reforma de la terraza de la casa de ambos en Figaro Street. El resultado es un espacio que posee el encanto de un artista varón algo descuidado, pero suavizado por la sensibilidad femenina. Un elemento que determina el diseño es el suelo negro: una base monolítica que se extiende desde el porche delantero hasta la zona del comedor. Otro rasgo característico es el aislamiento o, mejor dicho, la falta de él, en el dormitorio. Esta pieza se abre imperturbablemente al salón, delimitada solamente por mamparas deslizantes de cristal y por cortinas. Sin embargo, la intención de esta falta de segregación visual no era el voyeurismo, sino la eliminación de las restricciones espaciales claustrofóbicas.

Cu Fua, con l'aiuto della moglie, si è occupato del restauro della loro casetta a schiera a Figaro Street. Il risultato è stato uno spazio con lo scarmigliato charme di un artista uomo, moderato però dalla sensibilità femminile. Un elemento architettonico essenziale è il pavimento nero: una base monolitica che si stende dall'ingresso alla zona pranzo. Un'altra caratteristica sono le pareti della camera da letto, o meglio la loro mancanza. Essa si apre tranquillamente nel soggiorno, divisa da esso solo da pannelli scorrevoli in vetro e tende. Questa mancanza di barriere visuali non è stata però dettata da un desiderio voyeristico, bensì semplicemente dal desiderio di alleviare la sensazione claustrofobica di spazi troppo stretti.

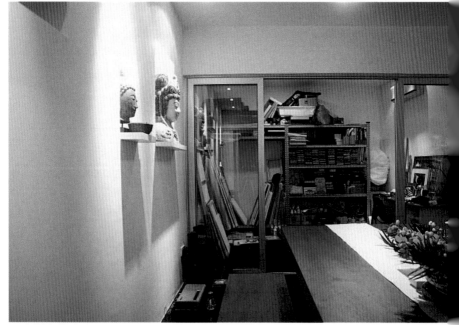

fortredale apartment

Spatial restraint is often a problem in apartments. Moveable horizontal and vertical screens have been employed to create expansive lines of sight and give spaces a dual function.

apartamento en fortredale

La restricción espacial es, a menudo, un problema en los apartamentos. Se han utilizado pantallas articulables en sentido horizontal y vertical para crear líneas de visión abiertas y dotar a los espacios de una doble función.

appartamento fortendale

Gli spazi troppo angusti sono, negli appartamenti, spesso un problema. Pannelli scorrevoli orizzontalmente o anche verticalmente sono stati usati per creare visuali più ampie e dare agli spazi una doppia funzione.

PROJECT LOCATION **FORT ROAD, SINGAPORE**
FLOOR AREA **1600 SQFT / 149 SQM**
ARCHITECT / DESIGNER **WHIZ CONCEPTS**
PHOTOGRAPHER **KELLEY CHENG**
TEXT **NARELLE YABUKA**

In this particular case the designers were asked to create more space within the boundary of the apartment. In the original plan, the apartment was compartmentalised into three bedrooms, a living-cum-dining area, a kitchen and other utilities. After reconfiguration, one of the bedrooms was merged with the adjacent master bedroom, and the dining area has been brought into the kitchen space.

A los diseñadores se les pidió que crearan más espacio dentro de los límites de este apartamento. En el plano original, el apartamento estaba dividido en tres dormitorios, un salón-comedor, una cocina y otros cuartos auxiliares. Después de la reforma, uno de los dormitorios había sido unido al dormitorio principal adyacente, y la zona del comedor se había ampliado incluyendo la cocina.

Era stato chiesto ai designer di ampliare lo spazio all'interno dell'appartamento. Nella sua pianta originaria esso era diviso in tre camere da letto, una zona soggiorno-pranzo, una cucina e altri servizi. Dopo la riconfigurazione, una camera da letto era stata incorporata nella camera da letto principale accanto, e la zona pranzo era stata portata in cucina.

ghim moh flat

The «house cleaning» process of the renovation has changed the original layout through elimination, reconstruction and a tinge of innovation.

piso en ghim moh

El proceso de «saneamiento» de la casa durante su reforma cambió la distribución original a través de la eliminación, la reconstrucción y un toque de innovación.

appartmento ghim moh

Il processo di «ripulitura» della casa attraverso il suo restauro ne ha trasformato l'aspetto originale grazie a eliminazione, ricostruzione e un tocco di innovazione.

PROJECT LOCATION **GHIM MOH, SINGAPORE**
FLOOR AREA **1240 SQFT / 115 SQM**
ARCHITECT / DESIGNER **WHIZ CONCEPTS**
PHOTOGRAPHER **KELLEY CHENG**
TEXT **NARELLE YABUKA**

The whitewashed walls, white ceramic tiles and beech flooring used throughout create an environment of calm and appeasement. Cream coloured seating and tables blend quietly with the interior envelope. Frosted glass sliding doors, softly transmitting light, further reflect the idea of calm and repose that had been sought. Clarity and uniformity is reinforced by the creation of recesses and wall niches to store the television, and to display decorative items. Mirrors are employed for visual enhancement of the space. They are particularly effective on a raised niche in the ceiling of the dining room; here, they take on the appearance of skylight, and significantly lighten the room with their reflection of white and light. A timber ledge along one wall in the dining room acts as both a display shelf and as a punctuation mark in the enveloping white interior.

Las paredes encaladas, las baldosas blancas de cerámica y el entarimado del suelo con madera de haya que se ha utilizado en todo el piso crean un ambiente de calma y tranquilidad. El color crema de los asientos y de las mesas combinan silenciosamente con el revestimiento del interior. Las puertas correderas de cristal esmerilado, además de dejar pasar la luz suavemente, reflejan la buscada idea de calma y reposo. La claridad y la uniformidad se refuerzan con la creación de huecos y hornacinas para guardar la televisión y exhibir los elementos decorativos. Los espejos se utilizan para intensificar visualmente los espacios, y son especialmente eficaces en una hornacina que se ha construido en el comedor, donde los espejos toman el aspecto de un tragaluz y con sus reflejos de luz y claridad iluminan de forma significativa la habitación. Una repisa de madera a lo largo de una de las paredes del comedor actúa como estante decorativo y como elemento de contraste con el revestimiento blanco del interior.

Le pareti imbiancate e i pavimenti con piastrelle di ceramica bianca e faggio creano in tutta la casa una sensazione di calma e pace. Sedie e tavoli color panna si fondono dolcemente con l'ambiente. Porte scorrevoli in vetro satinato, lasciano dolcemente entrare la luce e in più riflettono l'atmosfera di calma e riposo che si ricercava. Chiarezza e uniformità sono rinforzate dalla creazione di nicchie e cavità alle pareti per il televisore o per soprammobili decorativi. Per dare la sensazione di spazi più ampi si è ricorso anche all'uso di specchi. Un effetto particolare hanno per esempio quelli posti in una nicchia rialzata al soffitto della zona pranzo; come dei lucernari, illuminano significativamente la stanza con i loro riflessi di bianco e luce. Una tavola in legno lungo una parete della sala da pranzo funge sia da ripiano per oggetti che da punto di riferimento nell'ambiente, altrimenti tutto bianco.

house at jalan bahagia

This terrace house has some direct and surprising moments.

casa en jalan bahagia

Esta casa adosada tiene algunos rincones impactantes y sorprendentes.

casa a jalan bahagia

Questa villetta a schiera offre alcuni particolari schietti e sorprendenti.

PROJECT LOCATION JALAN BAHAGIA, SINGAPORE
ARCHITECT/DESIGNER RANDY CHAN AND JANCY RAHARDJA/ZONG ARCHITECTS
PHOTOGRAPHER KELLEY CHENG
TEXT NARELLE YABUKA

Randy Chan and Jancy Rahardja are budget-conscious urbanites with a penchant for good design. Randy is an artist as well as an architect. His wife, Jancy, is also an architect and together, as Zong Architects, they achieve a balanced design approach. The couple wanted their house to be a place where they could step back from their daily work and reflect. They wanted to be able to have their individual space within the apartment and they wanted it to be easily maintained. But perhaps of most importance was that the creation of their home would be a low budget affair. In fact, some unique features in the house happened as a result of constraints.

Randy Chan y Jancy Rahardja viven en la ciudad, son conscientes del presupuesto y sienten predilección por el buen diseño. Randy es, además de artista, arquitecto. Su mujer, Jancy, también es arquitecta. Juntos, como Zong Architects, logran dar al diseño un enfoque equilibrado. Esta pareja quería que su casa fuera un lugar en el que poder alejarse de su trabajo diario y meditar. Querían poder tener su espacio particular dentro de este apartamento que, además, debía ser de fácil mantenimiento. Pero quizás lo más importante era que la construcción de su casa debía ser barata. De hecho, algunas de las características excepcionales de la casa resultaron de las restricciones económicas.

Randy Chan e Jancy Rahardia sono cittadini ben consci del valore del denaro e con un debole per il buon design. Randy è un artista oltre ad essere anche architetto. Anche sua moglie Jancy è architetto e insieme, i Zong Architects, perseguono il loro approccio architettonico equilibrato. La coppia voleva che la propria casa fosse un luogo dove poter staccare dalla giornata lavorativa e meditare. Volevano avere un loro proprio spazio privato all'interno dell'appartamento che fosse anche facile da mantenersi. Ma forse la cosa più importante era che la creazione della loro stessa casa doveva essere economica. E infatti alcune caratteristiche, che risultano uniche, sono in realtà il risultato di risparmi.

kim tian road apartment

Ethereal and surreal, raw and abstract, this Kim Tian Road apartment combines it all.

apartamento en kim tian road

Etéreo y surrealista, rudo y abstracto, este apartamento en Kim Tian Road combina todos estos elementos.

appartamento kim tian road

L'appartamento Kim Tian road combina etereo e surreale, concreto e astratto in un tutto unico.

PROJECT LOCATION **KIM TIAN ROAD, SINGAPORE**
FLOOR AREA: **1200 SQFT / 112 SQM**
ARCHITECT/DESIGNER **WHIZ CONCEPTS**
PHOTOGRAPHER **KELLEY CHENG**
TEXT **NARELLE YABUKA**

The beauty of this scheme is that the apartment has literally been transformed into a piece of art itself. The interior is composed of three layers: a layer of cement screed on the floor, a layer of black-painted elements, and a layer of white walls and ceilings enveloping the spaces. A striking 7.4 meter plane of solid timber flanked by black mild steel benches forms the spatial and visual centerpiece of the apartment. Function-specific furniture such as sofas and chairs are absent. Instead, custom designed furniture such as the timber structure, a row of polyurethane foam, and concrete platforms provide open-ended interpretations for the users to explore and define the function.

El atractivo de este proyecto reside en que el apartamento ha sido literalmente transformado en una pieza de arte. El interior se compone de tres estratos: un estrato de cemento dispuesto por el suelo, un estrato de elementos pintados de negro, y un estrato de paredes y techos blancos que envuelven los espacios. Una impresionante superficie de madera maciza de 7,4 metros, flanqueada por bancos de acero negro maleable, constituye espacial y visualmente la pieza central del apartamento. Carece de muebles de función específica tales como sofás y sillas. En su lugar, muebles diseñados a medida como la estructura de madera, una fila de espuma de poliuretano y plataformas de hormigón, proporcionan interpretaciones abiertas para que los usuarios exploren y definan su función.

La bellezza di questo progetto è che l'appartamento è stato letteralmente trasformato in un'opera d'arte. Gli interni sono caratterizzati da tre strati: uno di cemento sul pavimento, uno di elementi dipinti di nero, e uno di pareti e soffitti bianchi che circondano il tutto. Un singolare piano in legno grande 7,4 metri affiancato da panche nere e acciaio dolce, costituisce il fulcro spaziale e visivo dell'appartamento. Pezzi d'arredamento con una funzione specifica come divani e sedie sono assenti. Al posto di un arredamento dal design tradizionale, come era già stato fatto con la costruzione in legno, una lunga striscia di poliuretano e piattaforme in cemento, lasciano agli inquilini il compito di indagare, interpretare e definire la loro funzione.

lengkong tiga apartment

Whiz Concepts gave this HDB apartment in Lengkong Satu a «twist of simplicity» by cleverly incorporating trendy understated design language.

apartamento en lengkong tiga

Whiz Concepts dio a este apartamento de protección oficial en Lengkong Satu un «toque de simplicidad» al incorporar de forma inteligente un sencillo y moderno lenguaje de diseño.

appartamento lengkong tiga

Whiz Concepts ha dato a questo appartamento in Lengkong Satu un tocco di semplicità con l'utilizzo intelligente di un design all'ultima moda, spesso sottovalutato.

PROJECT LOCATION **LENGKONG TIGA, SINGAPORE**
FLOOR AREA **1090 SQFT / 101 SQM**
ARCHITECT / DESIGNER **WHIZ CONCEPTS**
PHOTOGRAPHER **KELLEY CHENG**
TEXT **NARELLE YABUKA**

For Maria and her daughter, their ideal living space is one that is stylish, simple and practical. Carefully avoiding the term «Minimalism», Maria's brief was to create a straightforward and practical design that would be simple to maintain and easy to clean. With little opportunity to cook at home, Maria requested that the kitchen was kept nifty and minimal. Besides these basic requirements, the rest was left to the ingenuity of the designers of the project, Whiz Concepts.

Para Maria y su hija, el espacio ideal para vivir debe ser elegante, sencillo y práctico. Evitando cuidadosamente el término «minimalismo», el encargo de Maria consistía en crear una casa de diseño sencillo y práctico, que fuera fácil de mantener y de limpiar. Debido a las escasas ocasiones para cocinar en casa, Maria pidió que la cocina fuera elegante y pequeña. Aparte de estos requisitos básicos, el resto se dejaba a la imaginación de los diseñadores del proyecto, Whiz Concepts.

Per Maria e sua figlia lo spazio abitativo ideale ha stile, è semplice e pratico. Evitando accortamente il termine «minimalismo», ciò che Maria richiese era un design semplice e pratico, facile da mantenere e pulire. Con poche occasioni di cucinare a casa, Maria volle la cucina bella e minimale. A parte queste richieste base, il resto fu lasciato all'ingeniosità dei designer di Whiz Concepts.

moulmein road apartment

The physical form and delicate poetic capacity of the lantern have been translated into liveable space, which breathes light and advocates the philosophical.

apartamento en moulmein road

La forma y la delicada capacidad poética del farol se han traducido en un espacio habitable que respira luz y sugiere tranquilidad.

appartamento a moulmein road

La forma esteriore e la poesia delle lanterne sono state trasposte in uno spazio abitativo, che emana luce e evoca un qualcosa di filosofico.

PROJECT LOCATION **MOULMEIN ROAD, SINGAPORE**
FLOOR AREA: **1200 SQFT / 112 SQM**
ARCHITECT/DESIGNER **BENJAMIN KIM/THE MATCHBOX**
PHOTOGRAPHER **KELLEY CHENG**
TEXT **NARELLE YABUKA**

Skins of clear and frosted glass, breathing light in all manners – sharp, gentle, bright and soft – weave around the apartment with timber planes, carving space and directing the eye. The ribbed timber and glass composition that encloses the master bedroom, inspired by a traditional paper lantern, forms a focal point in the narrow living/dining space. When the bedroom is illuminated, a soft, seductive glow radiates through this lantern wall, and the public areas of the apartment resonate with pure lightness. Complimenting this lantern, is an assemblage of timber cladding and sliding doors, which wrap the walls of the master bedroom.

Las superficies claras y esmeriladas del cristal que emiten luz de diferentes formas – intensa, delicada, brillante y suave – serpentean, junto con las superficies de madera, por todo el apartamento, cincelando el espacio y dirigiendo la mirada. La composición de madera estriada y cristal que rodea el dormitorio principal, inspirado en un farol de papel tradicional, constituye el centro de atención en el espacio que une el comedor con el salón. Cuando se ilumina el dormitorio, un resplandor suave y seductor atraviesa las paredes de papel de esta habitación-farol y las zonas públicas del apartamento resuenan con una claridad pura. El revestimiento de madera y las puertas correderas que cubren las paredes del dormitorio complementan este farol.

Rivestimenti in vetro trasparente e satinato, che emanano luce di ogni tipo, tagliente, delicata, chiara e soffusa, si insinuano in tutto l'appartamento insieme a piani in legno, che scolpiscono lo spazio e catturano gli sguardi. La composizione in legno a costoloni e vetro che avvolge la camera da letto principale, ispirata alle tradizionali lanterne di carta, costituisce un punto focale nella stretta zona soggiorno/pasti. Quando la camera da letto è illuminata, uno splendore seducente si irradia da questa parete-lanterna e le zone pubbliche dell'appartamento si riempiono di pura luminosità. Questa lanterna è una costruzione in legno e porte scorrevoli che avvolge le pareti della camera da letto principale.

oxley rise apartment

This loft apartment has been transformed into an open space with distinct elements, inspired by the spatial music of Harold Budd and Brian Eno.

apartamento en oxley rise

Este apartamento con forma de loft ha sido transformado en un espacio abierto con elementos excepcionales inspirados en la música espacial de Harold Budd y Brian Eno.

appartmento oxley rise

Questo attico è stato trasformato in uno spazio aperto con elementi ben distinti, ispirati alla musica spaziale di Harold Budd e Brian Eno.

PROJECT LOCATION **OXLEY RISE, SINGAPORE**
FLOOR AREA **1100 SQFT / 102 SQM**
ARCHITECT / DESIGNER **BRENDA NG / WEAVE INTERIOR**
PHOTOGRAPHER **TERENCE YEUNG**
TEXT **NARELLE YABUKA**

This loft is conceptualised as an open space with distinct fixed elements. Using only a limited palette of materials in the design of the studio space, a dark brown, compressed-ply music centrepiece is held in a taut textual juxtaposition by the light-grey natural cement screed walls that surround it. White drapes, floating surreally, conceal the storage racks and help balance the boxy brown wooden closet opposite the bed. Daily essentials are deliberately hidden from the eye in cleverly designed storage spaces, achieving what the owner calls «invisible living». This visual elimination results in an interior space that focuses on real living, and not on mundane existence created by the accumulation of excesses.

Este loft se ha concebid como un espacio abierto con elementos fijos excepcionales. Utilizando sólo una paleta limitada de materiales en el diseño del estudio, el elemento central de la decoración, un mueble de madera de color marrón oscuro en el que se amontona la música, se mantiene en una tensa yuxtaposición textual con el cemento de color gris claro que se ha aplicado a las paredes que lo rodean. Las cortinas blancas, que flotan de una forma surrealista, ocultan los estantes destinados al almacenamiento y sirven de equilibrio frente al vestidor de madera marrón en forma de cubo que hay enfrente de la cama. Las cosas de uso diario se ocultan deliberadamente de la vista en espacios de almacenamiento diseñados de forma ingeniosa, consiguiendo así lo que el propietario llama «la vida invisible». Con esta eliminación visual se obtiene un espacio interior centrado en la vida real y no en la existencia mundana, que se crea por la acumulación de excesos.

Questo attico è stato interpretato quale spazio aperto con elementi fissi ben distinti. Usando solo un numero limitato di materiali nella progettazione dello studio, uno stereo è sistemato al centro, in una giustapposizione testuale tesa con le pareti di cemento naturale morbido grigio che lo circondano. Drappi bianchi che fluttuano in modo surreale, nascondono gli scaffali e compensano il colore scuro dell'armadio in legno marrone di fronte al letto. Gli oggetti necessari quotidianamente sono deliberatamente tenute nascoste agli occhi in spazi di ripostiglio genialmente progettati, realizzando la definizione del proprietario del «vivere invisibile». Queste eliminazioni visive, trasformano il tutto in uno spazio interno centrato sulla vita reale e non su un'esistenza mondana nata da accumulazione ed eccesso.

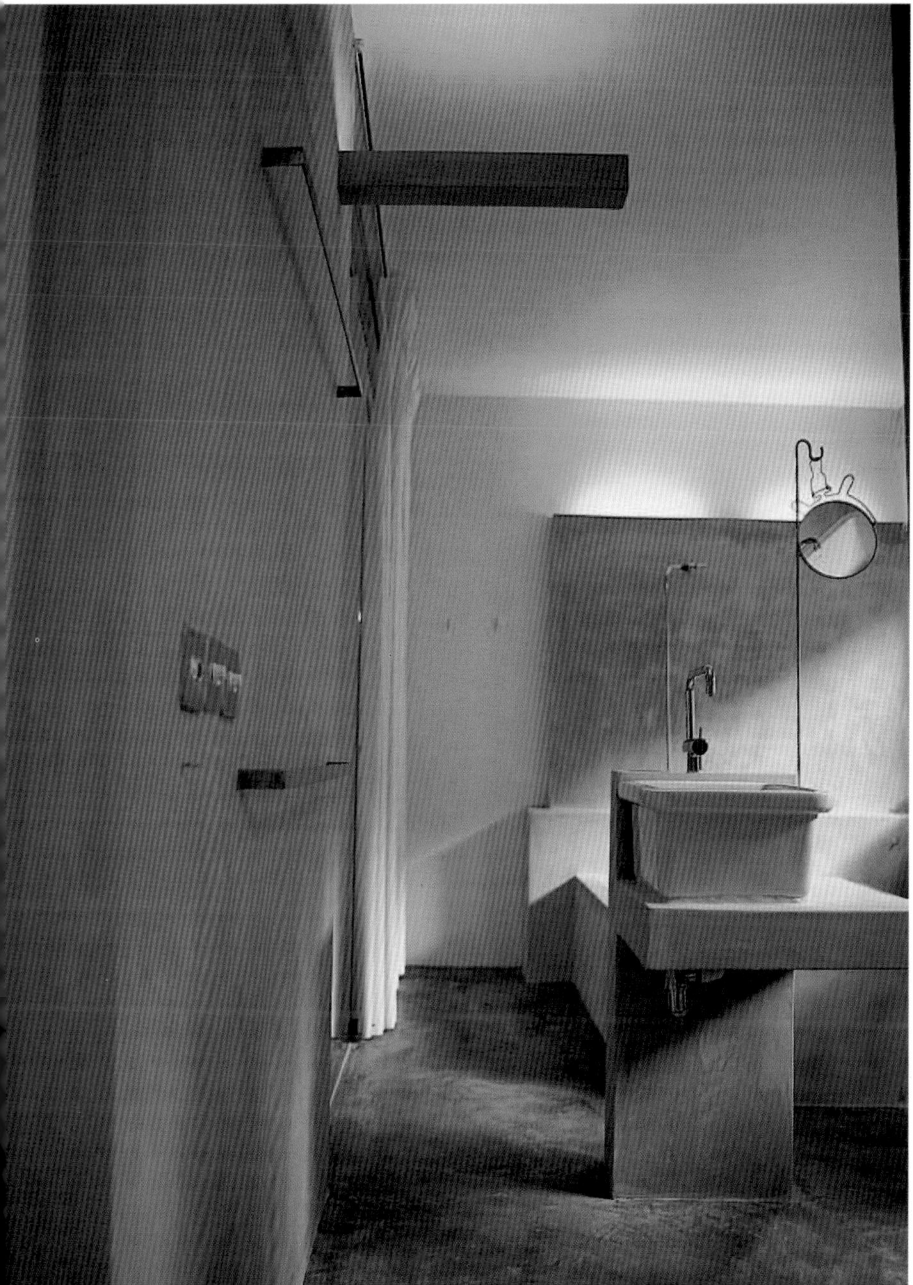

punggol road apartment

Plots and sub-plots compose this writer's apartment, with space sufficient and conducive to thought, contemplation and composition.

apartamento en punggol road

El apartamento de este escritor se compone de tramas y argumentos secundarios, con una amplitud que invita a la reflexión, a la contemplación y a la composición.

appartamento punggol road

Intrecci e intrecci secondari, come in un romanzo, sono alla base del design di questo appartamento appartenente ad uno scrittore, che offre spazio sufficiente e che invita alla meditazione, riflessione e composizione.

PROJECT LOCATION **PUNGGOL ROAD, SINGAPORE**
FLOOR AREA **1200 SQFT / 112 SQM**
ARCHITECT / DESIGNER **MICHAEL CUFUA / CU FUA ASSOCIATES**
PHOTOGRAPHER **KELLEY CHENG**
TEXT **NARELLE YAUBKA**

This is an apartment for a freelance writer who works from home. The designer, a close friend, was given free reign to design of his own accord, the only constraint being a low budget. He has created two stories in the apartment; one is a story of enveloping brightness, the other of accentuating darkness. The white walls, floor, ceiling and sofa in the living room are punctuated by dark timber elements – loose furniture (coffee table, sideboard, dining setting, bookcase), and built-in cabinetry. These concealed cupboards are of a deceiving appearance; they are detailed to be deceptively thin at the edge.

Este es el apartamento de un escritor freelance que trabaja desde casa. El diseñador, un íntimo amigo, tuvo libertad para diseñarlo, el único requisito era un presupuesto bajo. El diseñador ha creado dos historias en el apartamento; una es la historia de la claridad envolvente, la otra, la de la acentuada oscuridad. Las paredes, el suelo, las baldosas y el sofá blancos del salón se definen por los elementos de madera negra: los muebles sueltos (mesa de centro, aparador, mesa y sillas de comedor, estantería) y los armarios empotrados. Estos armarios ocultos tienen una apariencia engañosa; se han terminado de tal forma que en los bordes aparentan ser delgados.

Questo è l'appartamento di uno scrittore che lavora in modo indipendente da casa. Il designer, un amico intimo, ha avuto mano libera nella progettazione, con l'unico vincolo di un budget basso. Ha creato due «romanzi», uno che racconta della luce che circonda tutto, l'altro del buio profondo. Le pareti bianche, il pavimento, il soffitto e il divano nel soggiorno sono punteggiate da elementi di legno scuro, pezzi di mobilio (tavolinetti, credenze, tavolo e sedie, scaffali) e un armadietto incassato. Questi armadi seminascosti hanno un aspetto che inganna; sono progettati nei minimi dettagli per scomparire come per magia agli angoli.

telok blangah apartment

The idea of a box within a box is manifested in this HDB apartment at Telok Blangah Heights.

apartamento en telok blangah

La idea de una caja dentro de otra queda patente en este apartamento de protección oficial en los Telok Blangah Heights.

appartamento telok blangah

L'idea di una "scatola nella scatola" è rappresentata perfettamente in questo appartamento a Telok Blangah Heights.

PROJECT LOCATION **TELOK BLANGAH ROAD, SINGAPORE**
FLOOR AREA **1240 SQFT / 115 SQM**
ARCHITECT / DESIGNER **WARREN LIU AND DARLENE SMITH**
PHOTOGRAPHER **RIDA SOBANA / COURTESY OF WARREN LIU**
TEXT **NARELLE YABUKA**

To Warren and Darlene, the design of their own apartment was grounds for the experimentation and realisation of ideas that would otherwise have been impossible in the commercial projects that they take on at work. The main idea is that of a box with a permeable shell within another box. The external shell of the flat is the enclosing outer «box». The inner box is conceptualised as a flexible unit that has the capabilities to transform according to changing needs. A permeable skin surrounding this inner box defines a transitory space between the external shell and the innermost unit. Light and air are allowed to filter through the spaces while maintaining visual and contextual linkages.

Para Warren y Darlene, el diseño de su propio apartamento fue un motivo para la experimentación y la realización de ideas que, de otro modo, hubieran sido imposibles de realizar en los proyectos comerciales que realizan en su trabajo. La idea principal es la de una caja de estructura transparente dentro de otra. La estructura externa del apartamento es la «caja» envolvente exterior. La caja interior se ha concebido como una unidad flexible capaz de transformarse en función de las necesidades. Una estructura permeable alrededor de la caja interior define el espacio transitorio entre la capa externa y la unidad más íntima. La luz y el aire pueden filtrarse a través de los espacios mientras que se mantiene la relación visual y ambiental.

Per Warren e Darlene, la progettazione del proprio appartamento è stata occasione per la sperimentazione e realizzazione di idee che sarebbero state impossibili nei progetti a cui lavoravano per i loro clienti. L'idea principale è quella di una scatola con un involucro impermeabile, all'interno di un'altra scatola. La copertura esterna dell'appartamento costituisce la scatola esterna che racchiude il tutto. La scatola interna è stata pensata come un elemento flessibile in grado di trasformarsi in base alle esigenze. Una specie di copertura impermeabile abbraccia la scatola interna e costituisce uno spazio di transizione tra involucro esterno e parte interna. Luce e aria si insinuano tra gli spazi, e al contempo vengono mantenuti visuale e connessione contestuale.

ban suan saghob

Inspired by Mies and machines, this architect's house takes cues from the International Style.

ban suan saghob

Inspirada en Mies y en las máquinas, la casa de este arquitecto recoge influencias del Estilo Internacional.

ban suan saghob

Ispirata a Mies e alle macchine, questa casa appartenente a un architetto, denota la chiara influenza di uno stile internazionale.

PROJECT LOCATION BANGKOK, THAILAND
ARCHITECT / DESIGNER PRABHAKORN VADANYAKUL / ARCHITECTS 49 LTD
PHOTOGRAPHER SOMKID PAIMPIYACHAT / SKYLINE STUDIO
TEXT BURANASILAPIN & THOMAS DANNECKER

Prabhakorn Vadanyakul has a machine in his garden. An airplane, to be exact. The architect has had a lifelong obsession with all things mechanical, and airplanes in particular. He has been building models for as long as he can remember, and has been a private pilot for a decade. It comes as no surprise that his own house exhibits a stunning complexity of detail and craftsmanship. What surprises visitors is how flawlessly it is integrated with its environment – a lush, wooded site outside of Bangkok. «I want to show that nature and technology are not polar issues,» says Vadanyakul.

Prabhakorn Vadanyakul tiene una máquina en su jardín; un avión, para ser más precisos. Durante toda su vida, este arquitecto ha estado obsesionado con todas las cosas mecánicas, y con los aviones en particular. Construye modelos desde que puede recordar y fue piloto durante una década. Por eso no sorprende que su propia casa muestre una impresionante destreza y complejidad de detalles. Sorprendente para el visitante es el modo en que esto está perfectamente integrado en el medio; un lugar boscoso y de naturaleza exuberante a las afueras de Bangkok. «Quiero mostrar que la naturaleza y la tecnología no son elementos opuestos», dice Vadanyakul.

Prabhakorn Vandanyakul ha una macchina nel suo giardino. Un aeroplano per essere precisi. Per tutta la sua vita questo architetto è stato preso dall'ossessione per la meccanica, quella degli aeroplani in particolare. Ha costruito modellini sin da quando era bambino ed è stato anche pilota per circa dieci anni. Non c'è quindi da meravigliarsi se la sua casa esibisce una stordente complessità di dettagli e un'incredibile perizia. Ciò che invece sorprende chi gli fa visita è quanto impeccabilmente questa casa sia integrata nell'ambiente circostante, un bosco rigoglioso alla periferia di Bangkok. «Voglio dimostrare che natura e tecnologia non si trovano ai due poli opposti» dice Vadanyakul.

beaux house

Designer instincts saved this little house from demolition, and saw it transformed into a split-level playground for a family of three.

casa beaux

La intuición del diseñador salvó esta casa de la demolición, y se vio transformada en una casa de dos plantas para una familia de tres miembros.

casa beaux

L'istinto del designer ha salvato questa casa dalla demolizione, e la ha trasformata in un luogo di villeggiatura a piani sfasati per una famiglia composta da tre persone.

PROJECT LOCATION BANGKOK, THAILAND
ARCHITECT / DESIGNER PICHAI-THEERANUJ WONGWAISAYAWAN
PHOTOGRAPHER KELLEY CHENG
TEXT SAVINEE BURANASILAPIN & THOMAS DANNECKER

When the desiner and architext couple Pichai and Theeranuj Wongwaisayawan bought this tiny house in Bangkok, their initial intent was to renovate it just enough to be comfortable while they waited to find the time to tear it down and build a new house. But they could not resist their designer instincts. Renovations became increasingly radical, and they find themselves, somewhat unwittingly, in an unusual home that suits their lifestyle.

Cuando la pareja de diseñadores y arquitectos Pichai y Theeranuj Wongwaisayawan compraron esta pequeña casa en Bangkok, su intención inicial era reformarla lo justo para que fuera cómoda hasta que tuvieran tiempo de derrumbarla y construir una nueva. Pero no se pudieron resistir a sus instintos de diseñadores. Las reformas se volvían cada vez más radicales y se encontraron a sí mismos, de una forma inesperada, en una casa única adaptada a su estilo de vida.

Quando Pichai e Theeranuj Wongwaisayawan, coppia di designer e architetti, hanno comprato questa minuscola casa a Bangkok, l'intenzione iniziale era stata quella di rinnovarla quel poco che bastava per renderla confortevole, in attesa di abbatterla e costruirne una nuova. Non riuscirono però a resistere al loro istinto da designer. Il restauro divenne sempre più radicale e loro si trovarono, pur senza volerlo, ad avere una casa del tutto sui generis che rispecchia perfettamente il loro stile di vita.

gerd fabritius condo

Cross-cultural Asian motifs meet head on with high-end technological touches in this hybridised apartment for an expatriate living in Bangkok.

apartamento de gerd fabritius

Motivos culturales asiáticos entrecruzados se mezclan con detalles de alta tecnología en este apartamento híbrido de un emigrante residente en Bangkok.

appartamento gerd fabritius

In questo appartamento appartenente ad un espatriato ora residente a Bangkok, quasi fosse un ibrido, vari motivi della cultura asiatica si trovano faccia a faccia con particolari estremamente tecnologici.

PROJECT LOCATION **BANGKOK, THAILAND**
ARCHITECT / DESIGNER **RUJIRAPORN PIA WANGLEE, P INTERIOR & ASSOCIATES CO., LTD**
PHOTOGRAPHER **SKYLINE STUDIO**
TEXT **SAVINEE BURANASILAPIN & THOMAS DANNECKER**

In this apartment, an open plan allows natural light through balcony doors on opposite sides of the building. The main living space, which could easily be lost in the darkness of the building's wide floor plate, is thus turned into a hovering plane of polished wooden floorboards between two window walls, loosely divided into rooms by furniture and screens. A home office opens onto the main space, but can be enclosed by extravagantly detailed sliding translucent screens – an effect that combines a Japanese touch with just a bit of British high-tech.

En este apartamento, el plano abierto permite el paso de la luz natural a través de las puertas de los balcones, situados en lados opuestos del edificio. La estancia principal, que fácilmente podría perderse en la oscuridad de la amplia superficie del suelo del edificio, se ha transformado en un plano de madera pulida suspendido en el aire entre dos paredes de cristal. Los muebles y las mamparas dividen este espacio en dos habitaciones de una forma aproximada. Un despacho se abre al área principal, pero puede cerrarse a través de unos extravagantes paneles corredizos traslúcidos; un toque japonés con un poco de alta tecnología inglesa.

In questo appartamento la pianta aperta consente il passaggio della luce naturale attraverso porte-finestre ai due lati opposti dell'abitazione. La gran parte dello spazio adibito a soggiorno, che potrebbe facilmente essere risucchiato dal vastissimo pavimento scuro, è trasformato così in un piano fluttuante di travi di legno lucido tra le pareti occupate dalle finestre, diviso in camere semplicemente attraverso pezzi d'arredamento e pannelli. Un ufficio occupa lo spazio principale, ma può essere nascosto da pannelli scorrevoli traslucidi, stravaganti e curati nel dettaglio, un accento giapponese con solo un tocco di tecnologia britannica.

osataphan residence

The boldness and modernity of the Osataphan residence make it an especially striking inclusion to the region.

residencia osataphan

La audacia y la modernidad de la residencia Osataphan la convierten en una impactante introducción en la región.

residenza osataphan

L'audacia e modernità della residenza Osataphan la rende, in questa regione, una costruzione che colpisce particolarmente.

PROJECT LOCATION CHIANGMAI, THAILAND
ARHCITECT / DESIGNER **ARCHITECTS 49 LIMITED / IA ARCHITECTS 49 LIMITED**
PHOTOGRAPHER **SKYLINE STUDIO**
TEXT **SAVINEE BURANASILAPIN & THOMAS DANNECKER**

The Osataphan residence is a thoroughly modern piece of architecture – a surgically clean white box with an interior that looks not to the romanticised past, but to the landscape that surrounds it. It brings to mind Mies van der Rohe's minimalist collages, where an interior is represented as nothing more than the view from its windows and an art object that it contains. While IA49's interior demonstrates a Miesian relationship with the landscape, it is certainly not Miesian in its details.

La residencia Osataphan es, sin lugar a dudas, una obra moderna de arquitectura; una construcción cúbica quirúrgicamente limpia con un interior que no mira hacia el pasado romántico, sino hacia el paisaje que la rodea. Recuerda los collages minimalistas de Mies van der Rohe, donde un interior se representa simplemente como la vista desde sus ventanas y el objeto de arte que contiene. Mientras que el interior del IA49 demuestra una relación con el paisaje muy propia de Mies, aunque no así en sus detalles.

La residenza Osataphan è chiaramente un pezzo moderno di architettura, un'asettica scatola bianca con un interno che non guarda ad un passato romantico, ma al paesaggio che lo circonda. Fa venire in mente i collage minimalisti di Mies van der Rohe, dove un interno è costituito da null'altro che da ciò che si vede dalle sue finestre e da un oggetto d'arte ospitato al suo interno. Mentre gli interni di IA49 rivelano una relazione miesiana con il paesaggio, non sono certamente miesiani nei dettagli.

index
índice
indice

acknowledgement
agradecimientos
ringraziamenti

We would like to thank all the architects, designers for their kind permission to publish their works; all the photographers who have generously granted us permission to use their images; all our foreign co-ordinators – Anna Koor, Barbara Cullen, Kwah Meng-Ching, Reiko Kasai, Richard Se, Savinee Buranasilapin, Tatsuo Iso, Thomas Dannecker for their hard work and invaluable help; and most of all, to all the homeowners who have so graciously allowed us to photograph their beautiful homes and to share them with readers the world over. Also, thank you to all those who have helped in one way or another in putting together this book.

Thank you all.

Queremos dar las gracias a todos los diseñadores y arquitectos por habernos permitido amablemente publicar sus trabajos; a todos los fotógrafos que generosamente nos han dejado utilizar sus fotografías; a todos los coordinadores externos: Anna Koor, Barbara Cullen, Kwah Meng-Ching, Reiko Kasai, Richard Se, Savinee Buranasilapin, Tatsuo Iso, Thomas Dannecker, por su duro trabajo e inestimable ayuda; y a todos los propietarios que amablemente nos permitieron fotografiar sus maravillosas casas y compartirlas con lectores de todo el mundo. También queremos dar las gracias a todos aquellos que de una u otra forma nos ayudaron a realizar este libro.

Gracias a todos.

Desideriamo ringraziare tutti gli architetti e i designer che ci hanno gentilmente permesso di pubblicare le loro opere; tutti i fotografi che ci hanno generosamente concesso le loro foto; tutti i nostri coordinatori stranieri, Anna Koor, Barbara Cullen, Kwah Meng-Ching, Reiko Kasai, Richard Se, Savinee Buranasilapin, Tatsuo Iso, Thomas Dannecker, per il duro lavoro e l'enorme aiuto; e soprattutto tutti coloro che ci hanno cortesemente permesso di fotografare le loro meravigliose case, dividendole così con milioni di lettori in tutto il mondo. Grazie anche a tutti gli altri che in qualche modo ci hanno consentito di scrivere questo libro.

Grazie a tutti.